There Is a Difference

Also by Susan Seymour

Apostasy: The Deceived Generation

There Is a Difference

The Key to Discernment

Susan Seymour

WESTBOW
P R E S S®
A DIVISION OF THOMAS NELSON
& ZONDERVAN

WestBow Press books may be ordered through booksellers or by contacting:

WestBow Press
A Division of Thomas Nelson & Zondervan
1663 Liberty Drive
Bloomington, IN 47403
www.westbowpress.com
1 (866) 928-1240

All Scripture quotations are from the King James Version

ISBN: 978-1-4908-9250-4 (sc)
ISBN: 978-1-4908-9252-8 (hc)
ISBN: 978-1-4908-9251-1 (e)

Print information available on the last page.

WestBow Press rev. date: 02/12/2016

Dedication

This book is dedicated to my nephews and nieces: Karol, Jill, Katie, Jimmy, Josh, Ellen, Amy, Emily, and Elise.

My prayer is that you choose the right way and refuse the wrong way, discern between good and evil, and commit your lives to walk in obedience to the only true God.

Contents

Introduction

Christianity's current battle with nonconforming beliefs was brought to my attention in increments. I first encountered it when a surprising new curriculum was introduced in the eleventh year of my teaching at a Christian school. The "process" by which this new way of thinking was presented is discussed somewhat in Chapter 3. Later, I encountered the same doctrine in the teachings of the postmodern/emergent church and found them to be prominent in evangelical circles.

John MacArthur's book, *The Truth War,* brings to light error found in postmodern Christianity. The new "way of love" does not conform with Scripture's teaching, yet promotes itself as being the closest ever in "alignment" with God's agenda.

The "paradigm shift" inside Christianity is an organized, systematic opposition to truth bent on rewriting and reinterpreting God's Word. It is not led by any particular leader, but is a democratic approach which gives all opinions of truth equal endorsement. Submission to authority, especially valid authority, is its prey of choice.

Rebellion against God's authority is nothing new and even this current crisis in the church does not shake Him. Since the Garden of Eden, Satan has tried to twist God's words. This latest revolt, however, is very dangerous since it lays the red carpet for the Antichrist to prepare a platform for solving widespread global crises.

Rebellion within the church is currently shifting traditional church practice by first generating doubt through paradoxical twists, second, replacing fact with opinion, and third, redefining old terms with broader meanings. Its semantics urges Christianity to accommodate different perspectives and find common ground with other religions.

It promises peace and global unification. Even the elect (those you thought could never be deceived) are seduced with its rationale. Its philosophy of "at-one-ment" is only a physical remedy for solving human injustice. As it loves, cures, and mends, it is leaving a spiritual crisis in its wake.

Everyone agrees the world's teens (even Christian teens) are facing a critical future. This generation is on the edge of a fatal spiritual cliff. The battle line is centered inside the church as Satan mobilizes his troops to attack from within. His systematic propaganda has grayed lines between truth and lies resulting in vast uncertainty. Discernment has been the casualty. When a generation does not know the difference between right and wrong, and thus does not recognize the ambiguity between the true Messiah versus a usurper, it is the generation duped into voting in its own demise.

As a con artist wants to deceive people into buying a fake product, he banks on his victim not knowing *the difference* between his product and the real thing. In the same sense, Satan peddles an untrue interpretation of God's Word (inside Christianity) hoping many will buy into it without realizing its fakery.

"Generous orthodoxy" is a church of all religions with enticing and loving slants that promote any road as the way to heaven. It reshapes God's love into a love that embraces evil. It promotes inclusiveness as a doctrine which includes even error. Cleverly devised and implemented, this "new rebellion" is conditioning a generation to accept anything as truth.

This latest revolt is the big one. It's wrapped in all the right terminology. It's the coup d'etat that will establish the very base of ideology needed to usher in the Antichrist as he "emerges" onto the scene. It's an insurrection that is so subversive and extreme it won't be topped by future uprisings. It is an intentional opposition to truth targeting Christianity and its only valid offer of salvation. It is relocating church practice from the rock to the sand.

Rather than preaching from the perspective that Christian under-pinnings must be repaired, the progressive/pragmatic church tells us that fundamental principles have only held us back and must be discarded. While the church has half-heartedly watched outside her walls for danger, this hazardous threat has sprung up and taken root right under her nose. Children raised in Christian churches over the last twenty years are the ones leading the revolt.

This wavering generation has been marked by Satan to lead his assault. He has blurred the lines between right and wrong for decades in order to erase discernment, conditioning society for his dictator. He wants zero resistance for his ultimate solution. Resistance is very low because he has cleverly packaged his philosophy in love and tolerance. It is directed at a generation groomed to swallow it. When a generation does not know what to tolerate and what to reject, it is the generation ready for domination and subjection. This generation is ripe to accept a beautiful package sporting a shiny red bow of love, but ignorant of the surprisingly devastating contents.

The arrows are specifically centered on truth exclusive only to Christianity. More than ever, Christians should be ready to defend the faith of the first church. As athletes go back to the basics after they face faltering results, we too, must go back to the basics of the Bible rather than seek a skewed new slant on love and peace. Uncertainty facing the world's youth has resulted from rampant disregard for truth and seeking to please culture rather than God. We must determine to resist the onslaught lest the souls of this generation perish with our complacency.

Strong deception has elevated because the return of Jesus is immi-nent. Truth must be taken seriously or this generation will perish in their cooperation with fatal new "revelations" of Scripture. Avoiding compromise requires learning key differences between the physical and spiritual realm and between false and true statements. It also requires discerning true content for its validity rather than its persuasive presentation, loving demeanor, or appearance of authority.

Current mutiny inside Christianity is no cause to panic. Even this current crisis does not change God's immutability. They are but signs of the times. As we see the fulfillment of Scripture, we are to be "looking for that blessed hope, and the glorious appearing of the great God and our Savior Jesus Christ" (Titus 2:13).

My hope is that this book will encourage Christians to stand against the Enemy's strategy. It was written to help Christians recognize the clever, but deceitful, half-truths which have invaded practically every source of information available. (It is a half-truth that shifts a person from truth to lie.) Recognition of obscure shifts in teaching comes from exercising our senses to discern both good and evil (Heb. 5:14).

May the faithful be encouraged to contend for the faith which was once delivered to the saints and is currently available to us in our Bibles (Jude 3). By reading the Bible cover to cover we become confident in what we defend. My prayer is that this book will aid in saving as many souls from deception as possible and may those who follow false religions turn to the true Christ as revealed in the scriptures of Christianity.

Part 1

Contradiction

Chapter 1

The Paradigm Shift

According to a popular Christian magazine, something is "brewing and stirring in this generation" and something "new and dynamic" is taking place in the church. The activism is a compassion-driven roll call for acts of social justice directed not only at mankind, but also planet Earth, as "90% of evangelicals support green environmentalism."[1]

The world is calling for all nations and all people to come together and share in the Earth's "glorious" natural resources, weaving together all faiths and ideologies. This interaction is said to ultimately usher in a heavenly kingdom on Earth. The call is so loud and persuasive that the churches are turning their ears to listen and lining up with other nations and creeds to participate in the great "paradigm shift."

A "paradigm" is a system, a pattern, or simply put, a way of doing things. Christians have used the Bible as their pattern since it was written. The laws and commandments of God have long been our guide for how we "do things." Nobody can easily persuade Christianity to abandon these truths and embrace another paradigm over night. But if given a decade, many in church can be motivated and influenced to slowly shift away from the foundation. The goal of those striving to dissolve foundational truth is to eventually bring Christianity into a completely different way of doing things.

"Paradigm shift" indicates a slow turning from one premise to another. It takes place through trends, practice, and repetition rather than one-time incidents. Lately, long-standing truth has been supplanted with true-sounding fabrications that use Scripture quite cleverly and even humbly. No longer is mankind's answer for salvation through the blood of Jesus (of the Bible), but a wider scope of salvation is now presented to include *all* of humanity.

Since I wrote my first book, *Apostasy: The Deceived Generation*, I have had several people express dissatisfaction with the course their church has taken. They've noticed the "shift" in priorities *away* from God and *toward* human-centered doctrine. They see the application of Paul's words to Timothy: "For the time will come when they will not endure sound doctrine: but after their own lusts shall they heap to themselves teachers, having itching ears, and they shall turn *away* their ears from the truth, and shall be turned *unto* fables"(2 Tim. 4:3-4).

Facebook, YouTube, MySpace, Twitter, blogs and other social networks invite us to listen to someone else's story. Mass media shifts our Christian paradigm from one of separation to one of "connection." The harmless act of just listening to other people has opened the door to other perspectives. As a result, Christianity has begun to accommodate various views. One prime time news program had a segment entitled, "Everyone Has a Story" stating, "No matter where you are from, we are all really just alike." Christians now listen without discretion. We have easily swallowed the new global mentality that we are all connected, ignoring the principle of differences, based not on color but on creed.

First, Christians became fascinated with stories in movies, even teaching lessons from movie plots in church. Now, the subtle shift has grown into a more intimate interest for stories from people from all backgrounds. Specially formulated stories point out similarities and ignore differences. In the world this method is not necessarily dangerous since they deal only with the physical realm and since people are alike on that level. But in the church, when we address the spiritual realm, we find vital differences in people's stories around the world.

When we listen to testimonies in church, there is common ground and connection in Christ as the stories/testimonies focus on the work of Christ in our lives. But this can be taken too far if the "story" of God as written in His Word is no longer our focus. Stories can divert our attention from the Bible and onto ourselves. The culminating result of fables dominating our time over the past twenty years is a prevalent lack of knowledge of Scripture (and its Christ) and therefore a lack of discernment.

~~~

Since even the elect are deceived in the end times, we have to see another perspective. Even as we have become focused on people, there is also a new fervor for the "story of Jesus" in particular. However, in many cases (not all), the information about Him is misrepresented because the emphasis does not always represent the Christ of the Bible.

It seems anything of interest from movie plots to secular song lyrics to viral videos can be called a parable in church. Just because a teacher calls something a parable or even uses a real parable from the Bible does not mean he applies it correctly. Proverbs 26:7 informs us, "The legs of the lame are not equal: so is a parable in the mouth of fools."

Young people who have not been taught foundational truths of the Bible, but rather stories from television and movies, are embracing skewed slants on Scripture. They complain the Bible is "irrelevant" because its stories are unfit for our current culture. Distaste for the narrow field of information from the Bible is growing. A new hunger for a gospel that preaches truth from *any* story and from *any* source (even other religions) is gaining ground.

In these last days, the attack on Christianity (truth) is like never before. We shouldn't be surprised since God warned us in 2 Thessalonians 2:11 there would be "strong delusion" in the last days and in 2 Peter 2:2, "the way of truth shall evil spoken of." The attack is coming under the disguise of a new and better Christianity which is one reason why it's so deceiving. This coalition for a new Christianity prefers other names that are broader and less defining.

The new rebellion's books agree more with each other than they do with Christianity. The new emergent doctrine claims to be the result of previous stages of history, consisting of prehistoric, ancient, medieval, modern, and now postmodern, each having built itself upon the previous concepts as new thought evolves.[2] The proponents do not believe truth was true from the beginning and therefore never changes. New Christian books clearly advocate non-Christian principles where evolution is "credible," support for Israel is questioned, and authors are "sensitive to the plight of the Palestinians."[3] They are sympathetic to liberal agendas such as environmentalism, "facts of science," women in leadership, and treating "homosexual and transgender persons with compassion"... leaving out any mention of abortion. Wouldn't you think a Christian book with a chapter on politics would talk about abortion?

~~~

In order for the Antichrist to gain world dominance, he must eliminate true Christianity and any loyal adherents. He attacks from within, a proven strategy, as we see traitor preachers praising the "death of Christianity in America." Even though Satan has always attacked truth, the Bible tells us, "Evil men and seducers shall wax worse and worse, deceiving, and being deceived" (2 Tim. 3:13). We are living in a time when there are more transgressors than ever before (Dan. 8:23). The church is now captivated by wolves in sheep's clothing. She is allured, not even considering Satan's weapon of mass destruction (appearing as an angel of light). Strangers are now leading the church away from the safety of the true shepherd.

In the Faith section of a local newspaper, an article entitled, "Dueling beliefs? Group sees vastly differing religions as complementary" opens the reader's mind to how "other religions strengthen their own faith, highlighting the similarities while making the differences a little less foreign."[4] Another article called, "Two faiths join for a meal," praised when Muslims and Christians "prayed together in peace and respect" ignoring the difference that only one group actually prayed to God.[5] God's Word is not silent on the subject, "Your country is desolate, your cities are burned with fire: your land, strangers devour it in your presence, and it is desolate, as overthrown by strangers" (Isa. 1:7).

If the local newspaper of a conservative, Christian region in America opens its doors to broader perspectives allowing truth in all religions, we can conclude the influence is far-reaching. Sadly, the effects of this fervent activism is even infiltrating faithful churches. The movement is subtle with an ability to fly under the radar as it humbly coaxes participation without any indication of its impending trap. A false notion of safety and the belief, "I would never participate in Satan's deception" has led a lot of Christians astray. Satan winks and assuredly pats us on the back when we feel invincible. (See 1 Cor. 10:12.)

Today's average Christian is passive for truth. The Bible tells us God sends "strong delusion" whenever we do not receive "the love of the truth" (2 Thess. 2:10). We must love truth and hold fast to sound doctrine like never before (Titus 1:9). Apathy is costing a generation their souls. We must be the salt preservative for this generation and refuse the spirit of the age. (The spirit of the age is what everyone does without question.) Who would question listening to another story, another prayer, or another view? It seems harmless enough just to listen, right?

As we lovingly embrace a more tolerant version of Christianity and allow flexibility into our definition of truth, we then welcome an infected virus into our camp. Given time, it will spread until there is no cure. What is currently being preached as real Christianity yet open-minded Christianity, is not the real thing. Even though parts are real, it is the falsity that makes the whole corrupt. The new gospel is so flexible and compatible that it fits everyone's view of truth. Its new christ presented as the real, more loving interpretation of the Bible quickly leads its followers into a deathtrap.

For the last twenty years, the church has followed culture and popularity. As a result, we have "shifted" from the rock (truth) to the sand (lies). Satan had the church in his sights for two decades. Now he is pulling the trigger as a message of peace and justice sweeps the church of America and Europe. When there is no foundation of truth, people do not know the *difference* when a lie is presented as truth. Physical signs of departure from truth are passive leaders, lack of teaching, worldliness mixed with godliness, a seared conscience, and hype in our churches. Now we see the devastating spiritual effects of our complacency. In my first book I addressed these physical signs. When I wrote it, I was concerned with Christianity's flirtation with the world. Now in my second book, I see Christianity in a full-blown affair with false doctrine.

In the first book, shepherds were still God's men, but were passive about protecting their sheep. In this book, shepherds are not God's men, but are wolves twisting Scripture to fit their own agenda. Satan has patiently calculated how to get Christians to live passively. He has convinced them they "are protected by the Holy Spirit" and cannot be deceived even though their daily lives are not lived separately unto God. In 2 Peter 3:17, Paul warns, "Beware lest ye also, being led away with the error of the wicked, fall from your own steadfastness."

Pray for your church as the tsunami of twisted half-truths sweeps Christian thought without resistance. A half-truth is very dangerous in that we readily notice the truth part, but ignore the fatal part. Satan has groomed the world for over a decade to see only good, "connections," and "relationships." I will admit some things are definitely connected, but we lack training and discernment in seeing differences. Knowing differences is vital when Scripture has been violated with other beliefs.

Saying something does not agree with Scripture and is therefore wrong, has been labeled "judgmental." Propaganda applies the "judge not" commandment to every circumstance. But *there is a difference* when biblical instruction warns *against* judging others when we ourselves are guilty of the same and *in favor* of Christians judging right from wrong, maintaining righteousness in a culture. Inside the walls of our non-judgmental churches, Satan has been able to destroy discernment, breaking down any walls of defense. He now easily presents his agenda without friction since it is judgment that would stop him in his tracks if we would only implement it as the Bible instructs. (See Jer. 5:1; 8:7; 22:3; 1 Cor. 5:11-13; 6:1-4.)

Many urge Christianity to join with other beliefs. They are very rational in their interpretation of Scripture as they "by good words and fair speeches deceive the hearts of the simple" (Rom. 16:18). Of course religions are similar and connected. But we must have a healthy balance of knowing similarities AND differences. We have to realize what it means to both compare AND contrast. It is unhealthy to see *only* connections and relationships. When connections are overemphasized, the cost is lack of discernment. Knowing vital *differences*, in many cases, especially spiritual ones, makes all the difference.

Chapter 2

Discernment

For this generation of young people, the entire world is focused on tolerance for all people, all cultures, all ideas, and ultimately all religions. We are inundated with messages of how Muslims are "just like us" as they eat pizza or love their children, but differences are ignored. Overlooked differences are devastating to our welfare. Similarities cannot be a good thing if differences kill you. We can consider world religions in their common quest to better mankind, but it's the differences when compared to Christianity that sends their followers to hell.

What is this difference when compared with Christianity? The answer is JESUS (as revealed in the Bible of Christianity).

A revised definition of Jesus, without Scripture, focuses on similarities of religions, avoiding discrepancy. False religion promotes Him as a mere prophet or as an example of sacrificial living. It is error to equate His "way of living" as representing Christ Himself, leaving out the aspect of His flesh and blood, and therefore the cross. It is by Him that we are saved, not merely by mimicking His actions (Isa. 53:5).

The line of differentiation between error and truth is sometimes obscure. Mormons believe Jesus is God's Son yet do not believe He is God Himself. The same error lies in the doctrine of a Jehovah's Witness. A person must go right up to the line of demarcation, past all the similarities, to find the truth. The line makes all the difference. The *narrow* way revealed in Scripture is even more confined than we thought. Exclusive truth lies at the very foundation of Christianity..... Christ.

Deadly heresy stands at the doorstep of every church. It is ready to overtake every man, woman, and child in every nation. Truth is its target because truth is the only valid witness against it. Truth manifests the fatal differences. Truth which is unyielding faces hostility like never before. Sadly, the front lines are buckling from constant battering. Nonetheless, the church must adamantly stand up for the Bible and uphold truth with an unshakeable "it is written" confidence.

By listening to everyone's "story," we have swung the door wide for tolerance to overstep its boundaries. With "harmless" tales of other cultures and personal struggles around the world, our resistance has lessened as we are touched by what we hear. The line between the two (personal story and view of truth) has been blurred without distinction. On one hand, it is our Christian duty to listen to others' interests and not put ourselves in the forefront of conversations. We are to tolerate people and their story. However, we are not to cave to divergent views of truth. Other cultures can be acknowledged and their food enjoyed, but we cannot ignore essential spiritual differences.

~~~

Young people have grown up in a world of "no wrong answers" and a time when people do whatever is right in their own eyes, living by their "own truth." The verse in the Bible which refers to everyone doing what is "right in their own eyes" is the last verse in the book of Judges. The next phase of Israel's history was to cry for a king in order to fit in and be just like other cultures. They didn't want the exclusive leadership of God anymore. Today, many are also dissolving Christian sovereignty to be just like other cultures.

Just like the book of Judges, our live-by-your-own-truth mentality has culminated into a cry for a global leader who will right all the world's wrongs. America is not afraid to be affiliated with other nations in this cry. (Interestingly, a commercial for the Olympics showed banners with "Go World" instead of "Go USA.") Christian nations must not be afraid to stand for righteousness even when the "international community" disagrees.

Since anything goes for truth, real truth is very obscure. As a result, a starving generation is gravitating toward spiritual poison. Anorexic discernment among many young adults causes them to chase hard after the world's answers..... which is the Earth must find unity through agreeable "conversation" (even with nations who have proven themselves to be enemies). Language which terms anyone as "enemy" is now seen as radical and ignorant. But when the enemy concept is removed, all nations, and therefore all religions, are discussed as equals and compatible friends. Integrated ideologies are now the norm and even said to be "stronger" with each added perspective.

Negativity

In order to establish peace, we are encouraged to "absorb negativity." Negativity is anything that does not agree with consensus. It is absorbed by being forced to agree, losing its separateness. If negativity does not conform, it is eliminated or cast from the group. Christianity disagrees with the common belief that other religions include roads to salvation. This is the very point of "negativity" that will result in future persecution for American Christians.

Satan wants anything "negative" to be laughed off, rejected, or diverted elsewhere. Truth is considered negative because its narrow view confronts what is widely accepted. Confrontation is the enemy to world peace because it is unable to be "absorbed." The *real* negativity we should recognize is that which disagrees with narrow truth.

Error infiltrating our pulpits (especially youth ministry) is not confronted as we ignore arrows shot at truth. In the Vietnam War, the US sought "containment" of the enemy instead of confrontation and defeat. This only prolonged the problem and erased any desire for solution due to exhaustion. Satan is hoping the church will eventually give up the fight altogether and allow his infiltrators freedom to invade territory outside their jurisdiction.

The Bible is now negative as it clearly disagrees and contradicts other views. If a person disagrees with the residing flow of thought, he is labeled "non-progressive." Funny how unruly crowds of sign-carrying protestors loudly demand equal rights for their sins, but if a Christian opens his mouth in protest, he is quickly deemed intolerant and judgmental. When the majority is wrong (according to God's Word), then the majority is what is truly negative.

There is a difference between the new definition of love which smiles at everything and the real definition of love which smiles at what helps people and frowns at what hurts them. Christians are avoiding confrontation because they have been charged with judgmental and negative behavior. We must remember it is Satan who is accusing us. Jesus disturbed the peace with truth. We must resist lightening the mood, making jokes, and laughing when truth is at stake. Pastors must stop avoiding negative topics such as hell and judgment when his congregation is thirsty for truth.

Many preachers avoid negativity, proud their church is a happy place. In years past, some churches may have needed a dose of happiness, but the pendulum, today, has swung too far in the don't-worry-be-happy direction as it avoids sobering truth which hurts, yet heals.

~~~

A positive attitude now is to agree with others "no matter what." Meetings between world leaders focus on common ground and ignore glaring disagreements about rules of governance. Countries like North Korea believe dominant dictatorships are best. Iran lives to wipe Israel off the map. The UN smiles and nods in agreement to avoid being negative. We didn't learn from Hitler as he deceptively promised to go no further with his conquests nor do we remember the ambitions of other power-hungry despots. I think men of the past didn't believe these tyrants were serious. Now we believe them, but are driven by the desire to bury our heads in the sand and ignore anything "negative."

I, too, am influenced by the world's mentality as I feel harsh for saying there are certain things we cannot tolerate and certain things we cannot bring together in agreement. But I must ask the question, Should we tolerate evil? Can we casually sit by as a neighbor cries for help because we fear confronting a problem? Do we close our eyes when our children are abused? We have to concede, there are definite times when we should be uncompromising in our stand against tolerance. This applies doubly to the spiritual realm.

The new positive way or "dialogue to consensus" goes so far as to "agree to disagree." Glaring differences are overlooked in an unspoken bargain to avoid particular subjects of disagreement. "Can two walk together, except they be agreed?" (Amos 3:3). The day will come when the area of disagreement will have to be confronted. When it is resolved with truth, true friendship can occur.

As Christianity drifts from godly moorings and follows majority opinion, those who hold to truth will be pushed to the outskirts. It is interesting to see Jesus' warning that human consensus naturally disagrees with truth (Lk. 16:15). The world, as a whole, will never convert to Christianity. (See Matt. 7:14). The church will never be effective as long as it agrees with majority opinion.

As the Supreme Court of the United States recognizes same-sex marriage giving federal benefits, and rejects the Defense of Marriage Act, gay couples boast, "Now we will be the same as other couples." Really? How many obvious differences are ignored? One man stated it just felt "correct" now that he and his partner were given equal status with real married couples. Each state's approval hinges on the few who disagree but finally cave to general consent because they don't want to go against a person's opinion of right and wrong.

People who are obviously wrong are now given permission to do what they "feel" is right according to their own morality gauge. This same rationale was used by many Nazis to defend themselves after World War II as they claimed they only did what they thought was right in obeying Hitler's orders. Validating ignorance has only lowered standards to an all-time low. "Thou shalt not follow a multitude to do evil; neither shalt thou speak in a cause to decline after many to wrest judgment" (Ex. 23:2).

If we could see down the road and use the same line of measurement the state lawmakers used when they voted in favor of gays, we could agree that if a person really thought killing his wife was the right thing to do, he should be allowed to do it. The "who am I to judge" philosophy (started in the world and becoming prominent in the church) has no stopping point. By believing it is wrong to go against another person's beliefs, we throw out God's Word altogether.

The false religion of humanism gains ground when people are given the right to do wrong. With surety and knowledge of truth, Christians must not shrink back from defending the line between right and wrong especially when the truth will help a person in a positive (not negative) way. A Christian must first draw the line in his own life before he will defend it. It is true love that addresses problems and it is not loving to allow someone to feel assured in their sin. Confrontation does not involve shouting and figure-pointing as the world has led us to believe.

Dogmatism

It is now "judged" intolerant for Christianity to profess to be the *only* true belief with the *only* true Word of God. It's even considered small-minded for Christian missionaries to proselytize. It is viewed as arrogant for missionaries to have intentions of converting other nations into *one* biblical way of thinking. Ironically, those against proselytizing have every intention of converting every nation toward their way of thinking. We must remember, Christians do not believe the Bible is true on the basis of our belief, but because it stands alone whether anyone believes it or not. It was the *one* way of truth before man was ever created or even given a choice to believe. Validity does not come because someone (or even the majority) believes it to be true.

According to John MacArthur, "dogmatism is the new heresy."[1] It is now considered narrow-minded to think Jesus is only found in the Bible of Christianity. Criticism is aimed against those who just "have to be right." I'll agree that whenever a person pushes his own personal views and pridefully "has to be right," he should change and admit error. But Christians who stick to truth and "have to be right" for the sake of defending God's name should not change or admit they're wrong. *There is a difference.*

~~~

Many believe Jesus and His love are equal in all religions. They have come to this first by befriending non-Christian cultures, then crossing the obscure line of listening to reasoning behind other religions. Reason is one of human nature's biggest stumbling blocks. People easily follow false religions for their human rationale, not their truth. False religions approach spirituality from a human perspective, but Christianity approaches spirituality from God's perspective. False religions' salvation is about what man does for God, but Christianity's salvation is about what God did for man. *What a difference.*

If a society no longer has foundational understanding of truth, who can persuade them with Scripture? If a culture doesn't believe there are wrong actions, how can they be convicted with evidence from the Bible? According to Charles Spurgeon in a sermon on foundations, there are several foundations that must be defended at all costs.... Jesus, the Bible, the doctrine of justification by faith, the fact God was made flesh (flesh cannot become God), and the work of grace. These are the very foundations under attack by a generation who has removed them from their belief system. These topics will be addressed in the following chapters.

~~~

Christian views now agree with prime time America. In fact, proponents of the "new rebellion" inside Christianity proudly spend their days watching movies, listening to social media, and playing with the latest inventions of technology. They are *highly* influenced by culture and its opinions. Their Bibles are interpreted through a blindfold of broad-mindedness. Scripture to them is deviated through a darkened lens of connectivity which does not see the importance of separation, holiness, and consecration. Satan's aim is to align their thinking with the global view that All is One and the same.

The phrase "All is One" is very dangerous, yet common and accepted. It is a belief among humanists that differences don't exist and similarities join everything. The All is One symbol (yin yang) teaches that everything (all matter) is connected into one divine, unified, living, breathing whole. Another facet of this error is that everything (at its very core) is actually God and is, therefore, connected to God. It points out that at the base of everything is a true "essence" or "authentic self" (believing this to be a "divine spark" rather than a sin nature as taught in the Bible.) The church cannot listen to its logic for we know the heart of every man is desperately wicked, full of evil, and in need of a redeemer (Jer. 17:9; Eccl. 9:3).

The belief that God is inherently within everything is also called Pantheism. It even professes that the universe and God are identical. Even though it can be compelling and persuasive to desperate people, Christians should discern the difference. Sadly, All is One is the dominant, prevailing concept underlying most of social media's language and is therefore permeating young Christian thought.

Social Justice

Young people in our churches who are missionary-minded and are pushing with unquestioned confidence for justice in the world *could* have the wrong ambition if they are only motivated by humanism and not a desire for salvation of lost souls available *only* through the gospel found in Christianity. If a missionary helps a person in need without caring for the soul, he is not really caring for them at all.... spiritually.

JUSTICE is now considered the highest good in many churches (and the world).

What does justice mean?

Fairness? Equity? The rights of all men?

Yes, from a human viewpoint.

Are people starving? Mistreated?

Yes.

Do countries, especially Third World countries, need help?

Yes.

Do they need missionaries who will not shy away from feeding them the gospel after they have filled their bowl with rice, so God's justice won't require they spend eternity in hell?

YES!

But the priority of many churches is: "Feed the poor. Help the mistreated. Be missional." Missional usually means: A missionary who is compassionate, loving, and helps right any injustice (contaminated water supply, vaccine shortage, poor sanitation, poverty, abuse, slavery, human trafficking, catastrophes, etc.). But the real mission of a *real* missionary has been removed....... that of sharing the gift of eternal life through Jesus' blood. Notice: Jesus' blood rather than God's love. It is His love that provided the blood. It's not the actual act of love (of Jesus or the missionary) that saves a person. God's love for the world was present before His provision for salvation was given.

The obligation of the youth "mission trip" has shifted. Global efforts are now designed to improve living conditions. But it is the souls of men who are crying for help. As the church scrambles to correct "crimes against humanity," Christians must maintain that answers lie in repairing crimes against God (See Zeph. 1:17.)

There is a difference of perspective between Christianity's new *physical* definition of justice: everyone deserves a good life with clean water versus God's long-standing *spiritual* perspective: everyone is deserving of hell (because of a sin nature). God is "no respecter of persons" in judgment (which is part of His justice). (See Acts 10:34-35; Rom. 2:11-13; Col. 3:25.) It's not that we are all bound for heaven until something or someone wrecks our chances. It's not that we are good in our "true authentic self" until it is ruined by the environment or our parents' neglect. It IS that our true self deserves hell (true justice)........ until we accept Jesus as our only way of escape. The true perspective shows God's love is even greater than we thought.

To say the cross is only a symbol of love without the aspect of judgment on sin diminishes the work Jesus accomplished. An understanding of the true definition of God's love includes the knowledge of man's deserved punishment as Jesus took our place. God was not obligated to provide a way out of our hopeless despair.

In the Bible, there are 28 verses containing the word "justice." In those same verses, "judgment" is used 22 of the 28 times. There are 10 verses in the Bible that use "equity." The word "judgment" is named 7 times in those 10 verses. Judgment is definitely part of the true picture when considering equity and justice. You cannot have equity without judgment. (See Isa. 59:14.) Knowing differences between these words gives deeper understanding to Scripture. Judgment is a decision and justice is how it is carried out according to what is deserved. God carries out His judgment with justice and equity (fairness). Jumping straight to justice without judgment results in presumption. An obscure perspective erases the importance of decision, softening accountability. (In most cases, "judgment" has been removed from newer Bible versions and replaced with the word "justice.")

Many proponents of "social justice" are in the transition phase and most assuredly have salvation of souls in mind when going to other countries. But if the missionary is under thirty, it is likely his priority is not salvation of the soul, but of the body, the culture, and inevitably the planet through generosity and kindness. He has been led to believe that the soul is already "at one" with God and doesn't need spiritual redemption.

How does a young person raised in a biblical church believe every soul is going to heaven when love, tolerance, and acceptance for everyone is practiced? How does he think any person of any religion goes to heaven if only good works are manifested? It is because he has been taught (without explanation) that Jesus received all judgment for all people on the cross for all time.

Jesus did receive judgment for Christians AND non-Christians, but *there is a difference* in saying His death applies to all (with no future judgment in hell) without their even *accepting* the provision. Accepting salvation involves accepting God's covenant which is more than merely accepting His love.

~~~

Collective "love" from all religions is what will supposedly bring peace and harmony to our world of chaos. Peace and harmony is the "salvation" and "redemption" young people seek. Heaven can then be established on Earth in the form of the "kingdom of God." (True in a sense, but differences in the "kingdom of God" and the "kingdom of God" will be discussed later.) If the church only offers physical love and care, without spiritual love and care, we only offer a band-aid without first cleansing the wound. We allow the festering problem to grow deadly.

When clever comments remind us that Jesus fed the poor, healed the sick, and was all about stopping injustice, we can agree. Is it true? Yes. Was that the MAIN reason He came? No. Was there a spiritual purpose behind his physical care? Yes. We must see the difference. According to 1 Corinthians 13 (the love chapter), true love "rejoiceth in the truth" of the gospel (1 Cor. 13:6). The Word is given priority over caring for physical needs. It is where the power lies (See 1 Cor. 1:18). We also cannot fall for the rationale that feeding the poor IS the gospel. We only fall for that if we choose some verses and neglect others.

It is important to note, reference to helping the poor in Scripture does not always refer to those who lack money. David, who was a wealthy king, referred to himself as poor. (See Ps. 40:17; 69:29; 70:5; 109:22, 31). The word "poor" can mean those who are humble and

21

persecuted (poor in spirit). (See Isa. 66:2; Amos 2:6; Matt. 5:3.) It can refer to those belonging to God and is nothing to cause shame or require change. When those in Hollywood help the poor in other countries, they are seeking to help those without food and water, not necessarily those who are "poor" and persecuted.

By reading the entire Bible, we see Jesus' main reason for coming to Earth was to grant a much-needed, yet narrow, way to the Father. He came to be mediator between man and God. He offered eternal life which goes far beyond physical life. Jesus offered the spiritual water of life that quenches thirst for eternity. Those in the Bible who drank physical water offered by Jesus, yet refused His spiritual living water, did not gain access to the Father. Not everyone who "supped" with Him received eternal life because betraying spiritual exclusivity was proof of disloyalty. Jesus did not come only to offer bread from the oven, He came to offer the Bread of Life. *There's a difference.* Postmodern thought offers a cruel remedy by only quenching physical thirst and hunger without any hope for eternal life. "Though I bestow all my goods to feed the poor, and though I give my body to be burned, and have not charity, it profiteth me nothing" (1 Cor. 13:3).

Charity according to the dictionary is "spiritual love for others."[2] This means first giving physical food, then giving spiritual food of the gospel. The assumption that salvation is only a physical problem, is a spiteful joke, yet not a laughing matter. The simplicity of the gospel focuses on salvation of souls. Satan has diverted our eyes away from man's true problem (enmity against God) and toward physical suffering. He has blurred the lines between religions and turned us away from the true remedy (Christianity).

In Acts 6, the apostles were criticized because the widows were being neglected. Notice their reaction: "It is not reason that we should leave the word of God, and serve tables" (vs. 2). They kept the priority of preaching and spiritual needs first. But they also appointed men to oversee physical needs. They did not neglect the physical, but preeminence was placed on prayer and ministry of the Word (vs. 3-4).

~~~

Hollywood actors are praised for their sizable contributions to the oppressed and afflicted in other countries, yet we do not mention their lifestyles which, spiritually, defy God's Word. Praise is also given to global efforts which relieve human suffering but ignore spiritual needs of those bound by false religion. The new shift toward "social justice" in the church is misplaced if true salvation of souls is not given relevant urgency.

Discernment is not easy. Many claim they are preaching the gospel of salvation through repentance so we ask no further questions. But many times the words "salvation" and "repentance" have been skillfully rearranged. New interpretations for salvation suggest saving the Earth's global community from physical starvation, saving the Earth from fires and environmental devastation, and saving all mankind from the narrow confines of one religion. "Repentance" according to the new gospel is when people "repent" of their long-held views of narrow truth and begin to open their minds to all views in order to achieve a "collective viewpoint" of truth. The new creed states that only through human unity and "collective energy" can we gain salvation.

A half-truth either redefines a word or misapplies the real definition. Be wary of accommodating additional meanings with long-understood terms. Don't shy away from accusations that you are old-fashioned, traditional, or misinformed. It's become popular (in our churches) to find hidden, esoteric, mysterious, never-understood-until-now meanings which only result in impressing human pride and straying from the certainty of settled truth.

Satan's main goal is to get all he can into hell. He cleverly attacks where safety is presumed (in our churches). Using up-to-date preachers with great personalities to lead his program, he quickly destroys the very thing that can lawfully resist his lies....... judgment and truth. His aim is at the very pillar of truth...... Jesus. Christianity is the only religion that offers the true Jesus. There is no other answer for salvation from hell, but the one revealed in the Bible. The way to life is narrowly confined to one text, and, tragically, very few find it (Matt. 7:14).

Nobody is good enough for heaven and everyone is bad enough for hell. If anyone tells you he cannot understand how there is only one way to heaven (since there are so many religions which offer the same promise), tell him that in light of God's holiness and man's lowliness, and the vast separation between the two, you are surprised there is *even* one way.

~~~

Several places in Scripture mention we should not forget the poor. James 1:27 states, "Pure religion and undefiled before God and the Father is this, To visit the fatherless and widows in their affliction." In Matthew 25:40, Jesus says, "Inasmuch as ye have done it unto one of the least of these my brethren, ye have done it unto me." Helping the poor is a major part of our Christian walk. Americans *should* be donating to the underprivileged who suffer from natural disasters, starvation, or disease.

But as calamities increase, we cannot get distracted from the real purpose of the Bible. Definitely, we must help human suffering, but our foremost mission is to meet spiritual needs. Jesus told us, "For ye have the poor with you always, and whensoever ye will ye may do them good: but ME ye have not always" (Mk. 14:7). When He changes the course of the conversation with the word "but," Jesus is saying, "Feeding the poor is good, BUT I AM the one that is important." The transition word would not be needed if physical nutrition was all that was needed. It would not be necessary if feeding the poor was equivalent to having Jesus. But feeding the poor and giving someone Jesus are not equal because *there is a difference* between physical life and spiritual life.

The best scripture to answer man's problem is what Jesus said: "I am the way, the truth, and the life: no man cometh unto the Father, but by me." Recently, this verse has been twisted to deceive even the elect. "The way" of Jesus has been re-labeled to mean action instead of access. So now, acting in love which eliminates suffering or cures disease, shows "the way" of Jesus. It is even cleverly disguised to mean since Jesus showed this way, it is actually Jesus Himself doing the work. But Jesus did not show a way, pointing to something apart from Himself because He IS that way. He pointed to Himself. It *is* Him, not acting like Him that is the very point of salvation. It is not a generic "loving others" that gets a person to the Father. Humanism (Pharisee-ism) is a doctrine of works which is in direct contradiction to the doctrine of justification by faith.

Jesus said in Matthew 11:5, "The poor have the gospel preached to them." Verse 6 continues with, "And blessed is he, whosoever shall not be offended in me." There is no offense in helping or caring for the poor. But it is Jesus who offends.... the spiritual gospel, the specific, narrow, *one* way to heaven part that is rejected.

Eternal answers are criticized, condemned, and completely left out of books and sermons of social gospel advocates. Even when a young champion for social justice stands up after a disaster and cries, "These people need Jesus!" he may believe they need love and care *only* . He may believe Jesus is revealed through acts of physical help. It is shocking to realize the *real* intention of some of these zealots who are making their church families so proud as they cry out for justice, but are really striving for global unification. Parents and pastors should be asking young missionaries detailed questions to reveal if their hearts are loyal to Christianity or to humanity.

~~~

The good, right, loving, obedient part of Christianity (taking care of the poor) is the sheep's clothing ravenous two-faced wolves are wearing to spread their social justice agenda. Cloaked in what Christians have always known to be right, they then seek to redefine our terminology. Jesus is promoted as a loving, peaceful, dialogist who *only* came to establish a harmonious planet regardless of right, wrong, good, or evil. The sword of division and truth which offends has been removed. Close attention to this agenda reveals a concern for planet Earth rather than any real love for mankind.

K.P. Yohannan, founder of Gospel for Asia is a missionary who grew up in India. He stated "social concern is a natural fruit of the Gospel. But to put it first is to put the cart before the horse; and from experience, we have seen it fail in India for more than 200 years." He continues, "Yet while I realized the intrinsic nature of the Gospel involved caring for the poor, I knew the priority was giving them the Gospel."[3]

In his book, *Revolution in World Missions,* Yohannan writes of his concern and "deep pain over what appeared to be a massive imbalance between our busyness with maintaining Christian institutions, like hospitals and schools, and the proclamation of the Gospel."[4]

One day as he spoke in a church in Victoria, Texas, he knew his subject would be controversial and he was "afraid others would think [he] was being judgmental or... a fanatic."[5] Then as he spoke, he felt prompted by the Spirit to "talk about the dangers of the humanist social gospel."[6] Since that day he has insisted we "recover the genuine Gospel of Jesus- that balanced New Testament message that begins not with fleshly needs of people, but with the plan and wisdom of God - 'born-again' conversion that leads to righteousness, sanctification, and redemption."[7]

He went on to say, "Any mission that springs from the base things of the world is a betrayal of Christ and is what the Bible calls another gospel."[8] It cannot save or redeem people, either as individuals or as a society. He explained how modern efforts "snatch salvation and true redemption from the poor – condemning them to eternity in hell.....as the subtle humanist lie places the accent on the welfare of this present physical life."[9]

K. P. Yohannan speaks with authority since he was raised in a country that has experienced horrible conditions of hunger. Yet, he is saying the problem is not physical, but spiritual. His following statement demonstrates his understanding of the need for *real* missionaries today:

> Modern man unconsciously holds highest the humanistic ideals of happiness, freedom and economic, cultural and social progress for all mankind. This secular view says there is no God, heaven or hell; there is just one chance at life, so do what makes you most happy. It also teaches that "since all men are brothers," we should work for that which contributes toward the welfare of all men. This teaching – so attractive on the surface- has entered our churches in many ways, creating a man-centered and man-made gospel based on changing the outside and social status of man by meeting his physical needs. The cost is his eternal soul. ....You can tell the humanist gospel because it refuses to admit that the basic problem of humanity is not physical, but spiritual. The humanist won't tell you sin is the root cause of all human suffering.[10]

Franklin Graham, president of Samaritan's Purse, has helped many countries in time of physical tragedy. But he says sharing the gospel is the primary goal of Samaritan's Purse. He said, "I want to take advantage of such opportunities to do everything I can to clearly, convincingly present Jesus Christ and His claims." Some criticize him for being unfair in taking advantage of people when they're hungry, cold, or weak. But he answers, "You better believe I will take advantage of each and every opportunity to reach them with the gospel message that can save them from the flames of hell." He adds, "If we provide suffering people with food and medicine and then walk away, what have we really done for them?"[11]

It is beyond human comprehension to fully understand how much Jesus cares for the poor, the sick, and the suffering. He loves all nations and races....... all people. He gave His life for them. He gave it so they could spend eternity with Him *if* they choose Him *exclusively* and understand the spiritual significance of His life and death. We must with undivided heart, follow the biblical Jesus, and not swallow counterfeit representations.

Chapter 3

The Postmodern Twist

A prudent man foreseeth the evil, and hideth himself; but
the simple pass on, and are punished (Prov. 27:12).

The assault against Christianity is not just in America, but around the world. The world insists there are no differences between Christianity and other religions and even no difference between the God of Christianity and the gods of other religions. The hostility even goes so far as to infer, as I have already mentioned, that there is no difference between the Jesus of the Bible and the loving "way of Jesus" reflected in all religions. As the previous verse warns, Christians must be prudent to see this error lest we simply pass by, only to regret it.

Misapplication translates the "way" and teachings of Jesus as literally being "the Jesus" of the Bible. It is false pretense to "act like Jesus" in order to gain salvation. Of course Christians want to pattern their lives after Jesus after they have received salvation. But this includes all His characteristics, not just being kind to others. We must include His confrontation of sin, His holiness, His rejection of error, and His obedience to the Father to name a few. The new tolerance agenda melts the love of Jesus into a love which agrees and accepts everything with a smile.

Anyone who is not afraid of truth will admit an apple is an apple and obviously not a banana. Anyone who is persuaded and even believes an apple is as much a banana as it is an apple, is not only wrong, but deceived. We cannot say apples are the same as bananas simply on the basis of both being fruit. That is too broad and general. In a half-truth equation, an apple and a banana are fruits (true), so...... an apple and a banana are the same thing (lie). It is the difference which narrows down the truth. Even more important than discerning between fruits, a person must distinguish between truth and half-truths when eternal consequences are at stake. (Notice truth is singular and half-truths are many).

We cannot call any religion "the way" to the Father just because it has love and good works. That approach is nonspecific. *There is a difference* between unity in Christ and unity in love or even unity in the human family (See Eph. 4:13.) There is only true brotherhood in those who are unified by Christ (the real Christ, not the newly defined "spirit of Christ"). Brotherhood is weak if measured only by humanness. Unity of diverse beliefs is a farce, especially when one of those beliefs wants the other one dead.

Many sly fabrications, which contain an element of truth, are not attacks on the surface, but attacks at the root of Christian belief. The objective is to restructure Christianity from the foundation up, annihilating its authority. This is stated without apology in many "Christian" books. There's no effort to disguise the extreme overthrow of Christianity. There is, rather, a boldness in advocating this new "bottom-up" approach where the superior influence of Christianity is cast aside.

Paul warned early Christians about those who preached a new gospel and preached "another Jesus" (2 Cor. 11). A new Jesus is exactly at the heart of the new compassion-driven Christianity. Paul also tells us about those who "corrupt the word of God" and are adept in "handling the word of God deceitfully" (2 Cor. 2:17; 4:2). These seducers are very clever and very persuasive as they distort Scripture to make it look like it could mean something it does not. A person must know ALL of Scripture to discern the deviations. This generation is the most vulnerable to forgeries because of its sparse knowledge of Scripture. Their childhood was spent in youth groups which only sought to entice them, entertain them, and be relevant to culture.

~~~

Repeated messages heard over and over affect human thinking patterns. This is the systematic process known as propaganda. The world's propaganda is so dominant and resounding that high-tech churches have adopted it as the gospel. The information and opinions which are spread to influence and indoctrinate all of humanity are now part of Christianity's language. It's a completely different approach (a seismic shift) from the true gospel of traditional churches of the past and the furthest yet from the early church of Paul's day. In fact, old-time religion is repulsive to a generation bent on re-writing truth.

In order to persuade Christians to embrace change, a speaker may point out genuine mistakes made by Christians. He leaves out any good examples just to prove the churches of the past were wrong. So, everything he actually says cannot be disproved, yet he slants it in one direction to make his point. His audience is then ready to embrace change since they've been persuaded practices of past Christianity must be discarded.

Examples of extremism in Christianity's past should not shake us from the foundation of truth. Past mistakes of faulty Christians do not nullify the perfect example of Jesus Himself. When those "concerning the truth have erred," God is still right (2 Tim. 2:18-19). God has not changed no matter what people have done. Hasn't there been more acts of goodness done by Christians than bad ones? Who would know if you only listened to those seeking to destroy Christianity's example. Christian failure is no excuse to throw out Christianity.

Songs and phrases from social media and television easily stick in our heads. Advertisers rely upon this influence of propaganda. As foundations of Christianity are under siege and phrases constantly batter truth over and over and over and over and over and over, we naturally shift in agreement. Humans are bent toward consensus and don't want to be marginalized. People are naturally weak in bandwagon approaches. It's a shame many even vote for the person they think is winning.

Current propaganda (TV, movies, social media) steadily and consistently combats the following fact: *Truth is truth and cannot be changed or renamed.* Tolerance for all views disagrees. Public opinion says truth can and does change with time, and that it can be called by any name or fall under any heading. What was once wrong can now be right and what was once right can now be the most destructive, restrictive, and divisive way to live. The world claims truth is whatever a person believes it to be. From this frame of reference, a person is never guilty of wrong answers. "Meddle not with them that are given to change" (Prov. 24:21).

It seems anything can be stated as true. On TV commercials, apples can be bananas, cars can be airplanes, and anybody can be Michael Jordan. On the surface, it's ridiculous and who really takes the time to analyze it? We are usually too tired to care. One commercial does no harm. The harm is when these vague, untrue statements are 90% of what we hear. Media messages are thrown into the air in many different forms, but at their base they are not true and at their base they have one message...... truth can be anything you say it is because all things are equal. I cannot waste the pages of this book with more examples, but only hope to open eyes to the tactics of the enemy.

Comparison and relationship (including equality) is given to things which may have no relationship at all. Repeated application of this method has impaired discernment. Our ability to recognize contradictions and incompatibilities has been affected. Throughout years of propaganda, people (including Christians) have been steadily stripped of absolute right and wrong thinking. Cleverly, the messages are applied to subjects that aren't important (like fruits and cars) so that any protest looks like overreaction. The Enemy gets two victories: He gently persuades listeners there are no wrong answers and then he ostracizes anyone who disagrees (Christians).

To compare two unrelated words every now and then does no harm. Why get upset if it's just a car commercial and not really that important anyway? But *continual repetition* affects thought processes, especially for children. We may ask, "What is the harm in putting two unrelated words into a relationship if we are not talking about Jesus or religion?" But it's the foundation of how we think that's affected. If children grow up constantly comparing two opposites and categorizing them as "the same," it deteriorates any resistance when they are asked to compare things of value such as spiritual things or religious creeds.

Electronic games, board games, educational books, recreational books, cartoons, and other programs drive home a false comparison technique. Not only are things compared, but they are identified as equal. (I've seen the game, Apples to Apples, but I can't find Apples to Bananas.) Children pretend to be any thing and coaxed to simply "believe" something can be true. Sure, if you try hard enough you can connect "cheese" and "sunshine." They are both yellow, right? If a person says they are not *really* the same, they are just ignorant and unable to use their imagination.

Some things in life are, in fact, equal whether in size, quality, or usefulness. But life includes differences which, at times, make all the difference. For instance, people are all born the same. But when they become His, they become different. Acts 10: 34 and 35 explain this:

> Then Peter opened his mouth, and said, Of a truth
> I perceive that God is no respecter of persons: But
> in every nation he that feareth Him, and worketh
> righteousness, is accepted with Him.

The word "but" makes all the difference. God differentiates between those who are His and those who are not (in every nation).

He accepts some and rejects others. Physically, people are the same, but spiritually, there are two kinds.

Paradox

The latest fascination for connecting opposites is sometimes called paradox. Here is when we must really know the Bible. There are truly some examples of paradox in Scripture. For example: God sees and knows everything, yet He is "of purer eyes than to behold evil, and canst look on iniquity" (Hab. 1:13). Also, Jesus is God, yet He is a man. Another scriptural paradox is man has a free will, yet God is in control. In spite of true paradox, we must be vigilant against paradox not backed by Scripture. Be alert if something is presented as true when its intent is only to make evil look good or good be evil (Isa. 5:20).

The dangerous new slant for paradox intends to join the believer and the unbeliever in agreement. Transposing two opposites where they are no longer opposed, or even where they *become* each other, is rebellion and divergent thinking at its highest. (Sometimes and, even more deceiving, is when true paradox is used, but the application is untrue.)

The popular yin yang symbol from eastern religion has significantly affected American culture as we embrace its way of thinking. The swirling black and white symbol blends everything (even opposites) into one unified whole. It literally means, "as is above, so it is below" including even the extent that God is man and man is God. (See Num. 23:19; Isa. 55:8-9). Christians should be using this symbol for target practice rather than simply passing by its defiance.

It's a fascinating trick to erase discernment and raise a generation on equal comparisons "flattening" the world to a level playing field for every concept of truth. It's a glorified form of socialism as it brings the upper and lower classes into a common middle. It scowls at competition (capitalism) lest some idea (truth) win for its superiority.

Satan has thought ahead to strategically level the world with no authority. He wants disregard for genuine, narrow, defining attributes that point to the real Messiah. Today's mentality is a seedbed for imposters as Satan quietly prepares his pseudo-Christ. Young people are well-groomed to believe someone can be anyone as long as he wears the label...... or as long as they believe him to be the one who will bring hope to the world. Resemblances rather than reality may make a more palatable gospel, but as it goes down smoothly, it will have murderous returns.

In our society, young people see everyone as a winner regardless of effort, speed, ability, or knowledge differences. They've been taught the team is more important than the individual. True to a point. But beyond that point leaves out personal accountability. Global mentality rules out personal competition and opts for working alongside others in order to achieve common goals. When I taught school, group work and group assignments were popular, only allowing the low achiever to ride on the shoulders of the diligent. The socialistic approach, as proven by history, only causes failure as hard workers quit from the extra weight added to their own. Satan's desire is for the diligent, hard workers (contenders of the faith) to give up so he can continue with his deadly agenda.

~~~

Technology is not evil, but in the hands of Satan, social media is used to propagate his plan. He must restructure thinking in order to set up a unified world system. History shows revolution cannot happen overnight. Satan's revolution cannot go forward as long as the obstinate Christian religion stands in the way. He is frustrated with unyielding Christians who believe "one" means one and cannot include others. The unmovable "cannot" part is the roadblock. He thinks world unity would go forward if we could just agree lies *can* be true. Then in a few years, concede lies *are* true. The belief other religions *cannot* lead to truth is the very thing hindering the new cooperative movement.

Jesus is *one* man who is *the* way and *the* door to the Father. The veritable Jesus of Christianity has characteristics specified in the writings of Moses, the prophets, the Psalms, the four gospels, and in Revelation, not to mention the rest of the Bible. He is the fulfillment of all the writings in the Old and New Testaments. He is the person Scripture designates with clarity. We cannot get by with "just knowing Jesus" without the Bible because there is another Jesus available to this generation who does not fit the confines of Scripture.

Recently, false characteristics have been applied to Jesus. He has been misrepresented in Christian literature to have other names and other "forms" not specified in the Bible. This misapplication ultimately promotes the Antichrist as the Christ. ("Anti" means "instead of" or "against.") Two spiritual opposites can never cross over into unity. It's difficult for me to face the hard truth that those deceived will be young people I now know. For the sake of this generation, we must contend for absolutes and maintain that only Jesus is who He says He is and no other can take His place. We cannot think we know Him by only knowing He loves us. We must know Him intimately through the narrow distinctions of the Holy Bible of Christianity.

Leaven

Another tactic used in brainwashing is something that has become very prominent - *listing*. What I mean by listing is groupings or categories of things whether by color, idea, place...... whatever. Then thrown into the list out of the clear blue is a word which does not fit. It can be a book with several chapters adhering to normality then one chapter is added to stretch your thinking. It can be three ways a scripture applies, then a fourth which is something you've never heard before. (Of course we are always learning things we have never heard before, but speculation without verification is different.)

For example: Ford, Chrysler, Pontiac, Chevrolet, tree, Buick.

Sometimes it's obvious, sometimes it's a little more subtle. A speaker may directly talk about a truth and then indirectly throw in an irregularity. Your ears perk up and you question, but then you brush it aside as you think, "Surely, he didn't mean that." Weaker people think, "Wow, I didn't know trees were the same as cars." Followers look around and when no one else reacts, they turn back to the speaker like a baby bird ready for another worm.

When the concepts "creation" and "God" plus "evolution" are all put into one speech, we think the speaker surely believes in God since he used the word creation. Yet the shift from one foundation to another is overlooked as evolution is given acknowledgment.

It is not always necessarily in list form. Movies use this tactic as they predominately have a good story line, then throw in something contrary to Christianity. When a concept is added which does not conform with the rest, it's a misfit, a weed. It should be discerned as the different part. It should be rejected. Satan gets his "pork barrel" law passed as he attaches bad things on the coat tails of good things.

Verbal objections to the incongruity is either considered a disruption, negative, or the inability to accept a new concept due to narrow-mindedness. As Christians, we must remember the principle in Galatians 5:9, "A little leaven leaveneth the whole lump" meaning: One bad apple spoils the barrel or one misfit ruins the validity of the whole statement. (I am not referring to minor errors, but statements which shift away from the true meaning of the gospel.)

Sometimes this motley listing is used by speakers or authors as they hope to pull their audience in the direction of their theory. The listener/reader is captured when the speaker actually says something true and then pressured when the speaker's diversion leaves no room for question or when the writer makes anyone who "just doesn't get it" feel like an old dinosaur who holds up society's progress.

A continual diet sprinkled with error causes us, and especially our children to be less sensitive. We get to the point where we invite the intruder for dinner because he is "one of us."

~~~

It's obvious to some, but not all, that the media controls the beliefs of America. I really think it would be impossible to go one day or even one hour without the message of "unity in diversity" being presented.

Think for a moment about the meaning behind that phrase:

Diverse things are one (unity - "the state of being one")[1]

Diverse things are the same?

Unity in that which is different?

Unity between those who are different?

The same even though different?

Agreement with disagreement?

One meaning in ambiguity?

Together with different ideas?

In one place by different paths?

Compatibility with incompatibility?

Oneness through many?

Completeness in disagreement?

Wholeness through change?

Jesus in all religions?

Salvation through all beliefs?

All roads lead to heaven?

The world has embraced this message as it preaches tolerance for all views. It agrees wholeheartedly that there is unity in diverse views claiming all views are the same. But the Bible says there is unity only in those who are really the same (in Christ)....... and different from the rest. So, the world says "unity in the same" allowing same to be different and Christians say "unity in the same" when same remains unchanged. *There's a difference.*

Unity and consensus are important in households even when different opinions live there. Lines are not so important to hold whenever unity involves non-spiritual matters. Diverse views on carpet color or ways to build a birdhouse are all equal and important (within reason). Family members should consider all views in order to live peaceably. Also, common ground should be sought in businesses. We should appreciate opposing perspectives when we are living daily life. But when the one view of truth is at stake, we cannot compromise and meld all opinions.

~~~

The young people now setting policy for our churches are following, without question, the views of the world because of indoctrination from electronic media. This book will not even give space to quoting how many times most upstart "Christian" authors refer to television, movies, YouTube, and facebook instead of the Bible. One even stated the Internet could not be destroyed.[2] They believe God has chosen to reveal Himself through Hollywood and popular opinion while the true "word of the Lord is unto them a reproach; they have no delight in it" (Jer. 6:10).

In 1 John 2:16, we read a basic description of the world. It is the "lust of the flesh, and the lust of the eyes, and the pride of life." The current high-tech digital age is motivated by, and thrives on, fleshly, visual, and prideful concepts. Technology's *opinions* should have no place inside authentic Christianity. The rogues seeking to supplant Christianity are discipled by a digital life not spent in God's Word. The rightful place for these advocates should be seated in a classroom rather than standing behind the pulpit.

~~~

Our environment is soaked with anti-discrimination sentiment. Consequently, Americans automatically relate discrimination with racism. But the word simply means to make distinctions. It can, of course, be applied to the realm of racism, but it can also be used elsewhere. Since children are taught discrimination is always bad and are told connection and similarities are good, they aren't always distinguishing fact from fiction. This one-sided curriculum is also found in Christian schools around the country. Discrimination (in the right sense) is avoided. Disagreement between certain objects, processes, and systems is shunned. It's no wonder children have a hard time learning since they are not taught clear, right answers in contrast to wrong ones.

Basic knowledge for bakers includes an understanding of different ingredients. Those who think sugar and flour are the same face unpleasant results. Carpenters know how each tool should be used. Electricians recognize differences between wires. Gardeners distinguish between plants. The more distinctions a person understands on a subject, the more knowledgeable he is in that area. Those who are ignorant of these subjects don't know differences because all the wires or all the plants look the same to them.

~~~

Temptation to compromise with silly comparison/relationships comes when we do not want to overreact among friends or family.

"Can't you just act purple for the sake of relationship? It's just a game." It's not we can never compare things for humor's sake or that's it's wrong to see legitimate relationship. But Christians should be aware, especially for their child's sake, that the world is taking it too far for the purpose of desensitization against an exclusive mentality and toward an inclusive perspective which includes evil. Someone should invent a game called, "This Could Never be That."

Comparisons are almost to the point of ridiculous and most participants in these activities may be thinking, "This is so stupid" yet are afraid to say anything. Somehow, Satan tricks us best when the arrow is disguised as harmless or when we are in a group setting and don't want to draw attention our way. Contending for the faith starts at this very point of contention as we must be bold enough to admit some things can *never* be related.

It is continual repetition that is denying reality for our children. They live with relentless overlap of mixing two things into gray. Mixed messages always confuse. They are unable to discern black from white. They are persuaded to be creative and even pretend black is white. Those who are best able to pretend are praised for being the most intelligent. We must see the risk. It's not just a benign play on words or surface error that goes no deeper.

Incessant comparison between two everyday items truly does affect our view of truth. When our brains accept the idea that a boy can be a guitar or a leaf can be a loaf of bread, then we are less resistant to "imagining" that Jesus could come as anyone other than who He really is. When we accept "innocent fiction" which tells us God can appear as a woman, then we are at the threshold of blasphemous error. Acceptance numbs us until we go so far as to acknowledge "truth" in other belief systems or even see nothing wrong in viewing truth from another perspective. But narrow is the way to life meaning God can only be approached through Jesus and Jesus can only be revealed through the Bible.

Yes, to accept truth in other religions is further down the road than just comparing two things in a game. Mature Christians who truly know Jesus could never admit He is in other religions. But mature Christians have had foundational truth without continual connection practices in their childhood. I could say, but with reservation, a Christian can actually participate in these imaginative behaviors without cost. But only if they maintain recognition of differences.

~~~

Consider walking in the mountains and seeing antlers sticking out from the trees. It would be ridiculous to argue there's only antlers and no animal. Even when camouflaged, the animal is evidenced by visible antlers. In the same sense, a continual connection mentality is the antlers signifying a larger "deer." The deer is the all-inclusive, one world mentality which will be almost irreversible in the mindset of those conditioned to believe it.

The relationship/connection explosion in our present media is the tip of the iceberg. The tip is the indication of a huge mass below the surface lurking to sink the ship of reality and our child's ability to discern truth. It's to the critical point a parent can plead and pull the arm of their child all day, yet be unable to persuade him from following the movement toward world peace. Sadly, most parents aren't even trying to pull their child's arm.

Imagination has been encouraged so that the line between make-believe and reality is difficult to see. If a child never hears truth is separate, more important, and more REAL than make-believe, he will never know the difference. Recently, children are taught that fantasy is real, even deepening their deception. Truth cannot be imagined. Its source is not the mind. Are we afraid of truth even though we know it's what sets us free? Satan is clever in shifting foundations to the sand so he can sweep away the house when the time comes.

Soft and Smooth

Ps. 55:21 cautions that an enemy's words are "smoother than butter, but war is in his heart: his words are softer than oil, yet are they drawn swords." Knowing that alone makes a person want discernment. Deception does not occur with a gun pointed at our face. It accompanies a smiling face that approaches us in the name of love, friendship, and brotherhood. If there were no consequences for believing lies, we needn't worry. But there are devastating effects, *especially* concerning religion and spiritual things.

Christians agree that the Antichrist's words will be smooth, yet the current smoothness of preliminary lies is ignored. The spirit of Antichrist is already at work. (See 1 Jn. 4:3.) The only way big lies work is if little fibs take hold. Now coexistence and tolerance are praised with fervor. Soon, the Antichrist's solution will also be praised, not as some sudden new idea, but as the perfect implementation of what the majority has already been conditioned to believe. Right now, majority opinion concerning truth, goodness, and world peace is being renovated on a daily basis through social media. People's views are cultivated by propaganda as they follow the crowd and partake of all that goes viral.

People will already believe with their whole heart what the Antichrist offers. His government will be a "democracy" of peace, a "regime of tolerance." He will be the precise agent to accomplish what everyone already thinks is best. His website will have millions of hits. His smooth-talking video will only be perpetuated by sitting ducks who gleefully tell their friends on facebook. The world and the false church desire to be new world citizens. The "harlot" church is without discretion. Only the true church will not follow the popular tide. (See Nah. 3:4; Rev. 17:5.)

If anything was ever smoother than butter or softer than oil, it is the extensive new movement inside Christianity. While the message "love wins" comes from its mouth, fiery darts are aimed at the foundations of faith (Eph. 6:16). Its new revelations claim to be real truth as it accuses traditional Christianity of misleading its victims.

In a book I purchased from a Christian bookstore published by Baker Books, I shockingly read the following statement: "Can it be that the teachings of the gospel are embedded and can be found in reality itself rather than exclusively isolated to sacred texts... rather can it be they are embedded in.... other religions?"[3] Using the word "sacred text" instead of "Holy Bible" is cleverly indirect if most of your readers are Christians.

We assume all literature is safe in our local Christian bookstore. But deception has taken a strong foothold under the "Christian" label. Shelf space is now wasted, as is the reader's time, as these books question truth and suggest it can be found in other religions. If a person knows the true definition of "gospel" as defined in 1 Corinthians 15, he knows the gospel of truth by which we "are saved" is that "Christ died for our sins.... was buried, and … rose again." The gospel that Jesus commissioned to His disciples was to preach Him, crucified and risen, and the repentance and remission of sins through exclusive trust in His sole provision (Lk. 24: 46-47). Since the foundation of the world, that has not changed. (See Rev. 13:8.)

Clearly, that is *not* the gospel found in other religions. We cannot succumb to new criteria just because it demands old things are obsolete and must change. The more outdated the Bible becomes with culture, the more it proves culture is sliding toward decadence.

It is primarily the youth who are wholeheartedly inhaling the new approach to the gospel. Youthful zeal can be verified throughout history. Lately, they are fired up about the justice agenda, per-suaded it is undoubtedly the right solution. They've grown up in mega-churches with hyped services, have seen money lavishly wasted, and they're tired of the shallowness. Now they're turning toward sacrificial lives with few necessities, hoping God is appeased for previous selfishness.

However, their foundation is not the Bible. They have built their religion on the only foundation they know...... facebook, twitter, video games, television, movies, i-pods, i-phones, i-pads....... majority opinion.

~~~

It's not just the unsaved, but the saved who are starving for change. Poor biblical nourishment is the reason for the hunger. Weakness makes the church vulnerable for a completely new, bottom-up renovation. "To the hungry soul every bitter thing is sweet" (Prov. 27:7). In other words, the church is screaming for a "paradigm shift" from the rock to the sand. Deception and delusion have come as a result of not being valiant for truth (Jer. 9:3; 2 Thess. 2:10). If we had remained true to Scripture, discernment would have refused the new dainty dish and detect its putrid fishy smell.

The world is chasing after change and the church is on her heals. Romans 1 mentions those who change truth into lies (vs. 25). If a person does not know the truth of the Bible and hears someone say, "This is what the Bible says" or "This is what the Bible means," he likely believes the interpretation. We cannot be afraid to question when we are confused by double talk that attacks absolutes. (Absolutes are facts that cannot pretend to be something else.) One area where I agree with the new doctrine is that we should question what we hear in church. The difference is between questioning traditional interpretation versus new interpretation of the Bible. *There's a difference.*

Christians must refuse to go with majority opinion as crowds follow "facilitators" over cliffs and into hell. Facilitators of brain-washing programs seem harmless since they lead indirectly. Instead of standing in front of the class, they sit among their trainees and appear meek and non-opposing. They, then skillfully steer people in the deviant direction they intend them to go. "Ice breakers" which bring a jovial atmosphere to current group meetings, are designed to free up participants so that skepticism is minimal. Who knew that in those moments of carefree group participation, Satan would be in the back laughing his head off until he suddenly shuts his mouth lest a bystander see his fangs?

If resistance occurs in such friendly settings, it is viewed as overreaction because people should just go along for the sake of peaceful relationship. How can there be underlying motives in such a lighthearted atmosphere? (How can there be a sword when the words are softer than oil?) This kind and peaceful atmosphere which lacks a dominant leader makes anyone who questions its direction "extremist" and thus an outsider. Many times the error is hard to nail down, but it is clear truth is never spoken. If someone has the nerve to point out this key factor, stand with him and offer encouragement.

Our questioning should not be done in arrogance or ignorance, but in respect to God's Word. We don't have to speak up unless it is a dart against truth. A lot of times, the facilitator is clueless about what is below the surface of what she is presenting. That is not an excuse for her error. But we must be vigilant and constantly praying for God's guidance in these matters. A good indicator is when the flesh does not want to speak up, but the spirit compels us. In these last days, deception is prolific if we only had eyes to see. It just requires tact in exposing it.

It is a carefree setting and lighthearted atmosphere that gives the enemy the upper hand because that is when it is *really* hard to stand for truth. Even then, we should not agree with error. One way of not agreeing is to remain silent or even leave. Pointing out error may be done privately, with kindness. Sometimes, though, everyone must hear to keep "the conversation" on track. If you're not in a position to correct others, just make it clear you do not agree. The only way we can know error is to know Scripture. We must not be guilty of arguing what we think is true, only what is truly true.

One strategic scheme of Satan in his quest to destroy Christianity is to pretend agreement with truth yet shoot down the presenter of truth. How tricky! As an illustration: For the past twenty years we have not heard disagreement with *what* Grandma says, just that she "preaches at us wearing a frown and holding a 10-pound black Bible." This propaganda stops any defense of truth because we do not want to be affiliated with this radical exaggeration. (In churches, I have honestly heard more criticism against those who carry a Bible than against those who refuse to carry one.)

Satan knows truth will ultimately be eliminated if he can rid the carrier or at least makes him/her afraid to speak up. If truth is undefended, it is easily railroaded by surrounding opinion and "conversation." Remember we will not stand for truth if we do not love it first (Jer. 9:3; 2 Thess. 2:10). Christianity is worth fighting for even when criticism comes from within.

The True Religion: Christianity

Recently, Satan's attack goes deeper. Criticism is not just directed at the carrier, but is many times aimed at truth itself. To say a Muslim is going to hell unless he repents is now considered "hate talk" not just to NBC Nightly News, but to Christians who have been influenced by postmodern thought.

In my first book, I sarcastically remarked that even though "religion" is a bad word in today's church surely "Christian" was still a good word, right? Little did I know, "Christian" was on the chopping block and next to be shot down. After first rejecting any affiliation with the word "religion," the new church is now ashamed of the "Christian" label since it carries with it the reputation of intolerance toward other beliefs. I not only read of this shame in several books, but saw on prime time television an interview with several young "Christians" as they shunned with disgust any identification with Christianity or the term "evangelical." The church wants out from under these labels because it is cowing to global disapproval.

True, Jesus was rejected by the "religious" crowd. But He was also accepted and worshiped by a "religious" crowd. *There was a difference.*

There is something the Bible calls "pure religion and undefiled" (James 1:27). The greatest men in the Bible were very religious in the right sense. We must verify that a person cannot be a true Christian without being the right kind of "religious." Zeal can go the right way or the wrong way. Those who are turned off by "religion" show a lack of understanding for what Christianity is.

Today's new definition of a religious person is a robot who ignorantly goes through motions to please God while looking down at others in judgment and haughty ridicule. That's the definition preachers are combating when they criticize the word "religion." But the real definition has never changed. It is a "system of beliefs"... that has a "powerful hold on a person's way of thinking".[4] Abel, Enoch, Noah, Abraham, Sarah, Isaac, Jacob, Joseph, Moses, and many others are commended in the Bible for their faith and their unwavering dedication to true religion (Heb. 11). Without attention to this major difference, the church has ignorantly thrown the baby out with the bathwater.

The Freedom From Religion Foundation describes itself as a national organization of atheists and agnostics. Should Christians align their sympathies with this agenda and claim freedom from religion? No, we must contend for the pure religion of Christianity and draw a line between false religion and true religion. If we have only relationship with God without religion then we come to him on our own terms through any way we think is right. It is the religion part that leads us to a true relationship with God. It is the boundaries and confines of the religion of Christianity that teach us how to relate to God (See Gal. 3:24.) Otherwise, we would need no Bible at all if relationship was all we needed. If Christianity is not a religion then there is no creed and thus nothing to defend. Satan would reply, "Exactly!"

There are two camps in our church today. Those wary of old-time religion and those warning of the new gospel. Paul wrote a very applicable comment in Galatians. "I marvel that ye are so soon removed.... unto another gospel: ...... there be some that trouble you, and would pervert the gospel of Christ" (Gal. 1:6-7). While listening to Christian media, you must know who is saying what. There are those who preach the true gospel and those who are perverting it. It is advantageous to know the difference.

We must discern which half is true and which half is untrue in well-stirred mixtures. There is a substitute that is passing for sincere Christianity. It is even quoting Scripture to rebuke anyone who speaks up in the name of truth or against its buttery, soft spirit. Be on guard for the new and improved Christianity that is setting the stage to place its "messiah" at the forefront of its glorious "kingdom of God." We must heed Paul's words to Timothy and "keep that which is committed to [our] trust, avoiding profane and vain babblings ... which some professing have erred concerning the faith" (1 Tim. 6:20-21). Do not fear rejection, but strive for the "everlasting gospel" which does not change with society's whims (Rev. 14:6). Jesus gave His great commission that we should preach "repentance and remission of sins.... in His name among all nations" (Mk. 16:15-16; Lk. 24:47). Stand for the established, unchanging, pure gospel and contend for the faith which the early church preached (Jude 3).

Chapter 4

What's the Difference?

> Her priests have violated my law, and have profaned
> mine holy things: they have *put no difference* between
> the holy and profane, neither have they shewed dif-
> ference between the unclean and the clean, and have
> hid their eyes from my sabbaths, and I am profaned
> among them (Ezek. 22:26).

It was the leaders of Israel who corrupted the holy things of the Lord.
It wasn't some outside intruder guilty of mixing commonness with
holiness. (See Isa. 9:16.) For the most part, churches today also are not
teaching the concept of separation and holiness. Commonness is reg-
ularly invited into the sanctuary. Mixing everyday attractions with
the gospel is justified in order to make it more palatable. Without
distinction, God is viewed as ordinary and thus, treated with irrev-
erence. The shame of this indiscretion is that it has been instigated by
God's own. It is even promoted as a good thing for the sake of uniting
Christians with non-Christians, erasing any differences.

Does the difference between holy and common matter? What about
between pollution and purity? Is lemonade the same as sewer water?
Is poison the same as medicine? Is roadkill something you want on
your breakfast plate?

Is holiness really common and nothing actually set apart?

Or is it even the opposite?

Is everything actually consecrated unto God, even things He has said are abominations?

Consider this fundamental pattern in thinking before you go further. Is everything common or is everything holy or are there differences?

Is it OK to compromise with a little filth? Is it even healthy for the sake of experience and so we can "relate" to others? Is gold enhanced when mixed with impurities?

Does purity rub off?

Or the opposite?

Does contamination contaminate?

Does a clean car splashed with mud make the mud clean? Or does the mud make the car dirty? The answers are clear and must be maintained in principle. We cannot allow Satan to erase these foundational truths.

Defilement

The church should be vigilant for the Enemy's intentions of polluting worship. Recently, gutsy and aggressive indoctrination has allowed tolerance to expand into the concept that *everything* has potential to be sacred and holy. Is there a line Christians won't cross? This concept is *spiritually* advocating an offering of broken, spotted, and lame sacrifices. "The sacrifice of the wicked is an abomination to the Lord" (Prov. 15:8; Prov. 21:27; Ps. 50:9; Isa. 66:3; Jer. 6:20; Amos 5:22).

Shockingly, the blurred distinctions between holy and common, dirty and clean, are intentional by many postmodern authors inside the Christian circle. In a chapter entitled "Dirt," the author writes that the history of America's religion has set boundaries and

> thus our dirt boundaries are also exerting a form of religious control over people-- telling them who is in and who is out, what sort of behavior is acceptable and what is not. It is my belief that the Emergent Church will be, as Christ himself was, a force for reevaluating dirt boundaries.[1]

Who is this uncircumcised Philistine that he should defy God and reevaluate boundaries which have long been established in His Word? (See 1 Sam. 17:26.) The quote is only the forerunner to the real message of the chapter. The author continues:

> I believe that Christ would criticize us for overseri-ousness, encourage us to lighten up and allow some muddy hands to grasp again our sterilized liturgies. To achieve this we will require tricksters to have courage, jump up with cheeky smiles, write their lyrics, do their part, play their music, and turn their tricks.... the tricksters must be coaxed out to help us find our dirt and nourish this tree, for our survival depends on them. They may not be easy to find, but one can be fairly sure that they will not be decked in white, waiting around.[2]

If one message is portrayed in this book, let it be that God is *very* serious about "dirt" (sin). His son died because of it. He will *never* "lighten up" about muddy hands grasping that which is holy and we can be sure that our survival does depend on our garment being white rather than muddy!

Physical dirt, as found in the field, is a good thing since we depend on it for food. Also, dirty hands, in general, are a sign of a hard worker. However, spiritual dirt and defilement are NEVER to be invited into God's presence. I am not referring to a sinner coming to Christ. I am referring to a sinner coming to God with his sin, without Christ. *There is a difference.*

Specific instructions were given to Moses concerning the tabernacle. As a physical lesson to teach a spiritual truth, maimed men were disqualified from entering the Holy of Holies. (See Lev. 21:18-21.) Not even healthy men who were common (not the high priest) could enter. In the New Testament, God speaks that in the New Jerusalem "there shall in no wise enter into it any thing that defileth, neither whatsoever worketh abomination, or maketh a lie: but they which are written in the Lamb's book of life" (Rev. 21:27).

Authors who intentionally mislead Christians into removing well-defined boundaries inside the church, are playing with fire as they encourage muddy hands to "turn their tricks" in the sanctuary. Sanctuary, by its very name, is to be separated unto God. "Spots they are and blemishes, sporting themselves with their own deceivings while they feast with you" (2 Pet. 2:13.) The Bible only praises those who have clean hands and pure, white garments. (See Ps. 24:4; Rev. 3:5; 19:14). God Himself wears a garment which is "white as snow" (Dan. 7:9). God forbid that church leaders stoop so low as to criticize spiritual purity and those who wear spiritually clean garments made white by Jesus' blood!

The same book also praises any art which shocks and mocks Christ's purity, all in the name of freedom. How did a book of such low caliber enter a Christian bookstore? How was it published by a Christian publisher? I'm starting to understand how the abomination of desolation (mentioned in the book of Daniel and by Jesus in the gospels) will actually take place. I just never realized it would be set up in the holy place to the sound of cheering. I had, instead, pictured the Antichrist bullying his way into the sanctuary as people fled in fear. I was wrong.

If the high priest had "muddy hands" on the Day of Atonement he would have been dragged out of the holy place and into a waiting grave (Lev. 16:2). Aaron, the high priest, had to have a white garment to enter the holy place (Lev. 16:32-33). It's strange what details Satan chooses to attack. Certain scriptures we paid little attention to over the years are very significant indeed.

Sadly, many pastors today try to persuade their congregation, especially newcomers, that they are as muddy as the next guy. They shun a separate, consecrated life and only see the importance of attracting the unsaved to church. That is a noble motive, but if the sinner is not taught the importance of becoming clean and different, we labor in vain. It is not an impure church that will draw the lost, but a church that is led by the Holy Spirit and His purity.

Holy requirements are also found in the New Testament: Jesus was the *only* acceptable sacrifice to God for man's sins because of His holiness. Also, God refused Ananias and Sapphira's impure motives by immediately killing them. Third, Paul told the Colossians to "stand perfect and complete in all the will of God" (Col. 4:12). God never approves, condones, or tolerates that which is spiritually contaminated. (See also 1 Pet. 1:16.)

Those who will be "decked in white" will do so with honor. The Bible mentions the privilege of wearing white. (See Rev. 3:4-5; 7:13; 19:14.) In heaven, there will only be those who are wearing white. Those wearing soiled garments will not be there. Any person who wallows in mud and then calls it clean is deceived because he does not know the difference.

The "dirt" chapter is a stepping stone to the book's conclusion. The author's successive assumptions flip flop meanings of Scripture, guiding readers into a paradigm shift. Without this method, he could never reach his intentions. If this book were some stray misfit why bother confronting its lies? Sadly, it is one of many designed for the last generation. The book's conclusion is in the following quotes about Judas:

"probably.... thinking that he had done the right thing and that Jesus would actually be pleased with his cunning plan, he strode up to Jesus and kissed him."[3]

This leads to his assumption that Judas:

"was the only one of Jesus' followers actually to understand the significance ..." and Satan entered him "because in horror the devil saw Judas' understanding and had to eliminate it."[4]

So, long-standing belief that Satan entered Judas because he agreed to betray the Son of God has been wrong? Are we to change and believe that Judas actually had the "real" understanding of Jesus. Was he actually the best disciple? The author says Judas' error was confining Jesus to a box. The confining box he means is the Holy Bible and Christianity. He feels salvation should be shared among all religions. In order to bash traditional Christianity, he writes, "We are all Judas" when we "pretend that Christ is located in one place or one person and that all who come to God must come in a particular way."[5] As a Christian, I am not pretending that Christ is located in one person. I will shout it from the rooftops: JESUS IS ONLY LOCATED IN ONE PERSON!

The author tricks the reader with the half-truth that dirt should be brought into the open, "from the dark places to the altar."[6] Yes, "dirt" should come to the altar, but it should be *left* there in repentance, then shunned and refused allowing a person to walk away clean. Rather, insolence wants dirt offered upon the altar as an accepted sacrifice. Rejecting dirt (anything which God condemns) by leaving it at the altar is different than bringing it to the altar as a sacrifice to contaminate that which is holy.

Isaiah warns us against treading God's courts with sacrifices which are abomination because He hates them (Isa. 1:12-16). Satan cheers when he is allowed to do "wickedly in the sanctuary" and bring his "detestable things" to God's house (Ps. 74:3, 7; Ezek. 5:11). His man, the "trickster" (Antichrist), will lead worshipers in whatever is off-limits. As his first priority, Satan in the flesh, will immediately head to the temple to defile that which is precious and holy.

Provoking God

Jesus will one day redeem *all* things, including creation. (See Rom. 8:21-23; Eph. 1:10.) "All" does not include irredeemable things such as Satan, demons, Judas, and sin. Death and the grave will not be redeemed, but destroyed. (See Hos. 13:14; 2 Tim. 1:10.) God will redeem the Earth *after* He melts it with fervent heat, removing impurities with cleansing judgment (2 Pet. 3:12).

Sinful man can be made clean (from sin) and holy through the blood of Jesus. But dirt itself cannot be made clean. Gasoline will never be healthy to drink. Mustard gas will never be recommended for use in a humidifier. Sin itself will never be pure and acceptable to God.

We cannot merely brand things holy. The works of the devil can *never* be consecrated for worship. His works will be destroyed. (See 1 Jn. 3:8.). Lies will never be true. Jesus cleanses us *from* sin and removes impurities as far as the east is from the west (Ps. 103:12). Jesus cleanses *from* unrighteousness. After a person repents, is converted, and his sins are "blotted out," he lives a changed life (Acts 3:19). Jesus did not come to say unrighteousness is now clean or wrong is now right.

Satan's intention is not only to make everything godly appear evil (negative) but to make everything evil appear godly. He patiently waits while the paradigm shifts and the language of harmony (between good and evil), community, peace, sharing, relationship, connection, unity, compatibility, equality, and agreement mix black and white into gray ….. persuading the church to compromise as it is facilitated from one foundation to another. John MacArthur defines the paradigm shift as "a wholesale overhaul in the way people think about truth itself."[7]

Those who are opting to shift church practice want to restructure everything. In extreme instances......... no more aisle, pews, pulpit, or preacher. It sounds so exciting especially to those who don't want affiliation with outdated practices. I suppose we could live without aisles, pews, and pulpits. But Satan will not stop there. He wants preaching scrapped. He would rather we "join the conversation" and "dialogue" our opinions. Preaching is the very thing God has established to turn unbelievers to Him. (See 1 Cor. 1:21). Question what is eliminated in your church and notice what is put in its place.

Crossing the Line

Definitely, there is a difference between right and wrong, up and down, left and right, safe and unsafe, etc. Sometimes the difference is only made distinct by a fine line, but the line is still there. For example, even though small, there's a difference between 104° and 105° in a person's temperature. There's a difference whether you're inside a cage with a ferocious lion or outside that cage. There's a difference in having a parachute, or not having one, when jumping from an airplane. There's a difference between burning a US flag and burning a shoe box. There was a difference, determined by Roman law, between thirty-nine lashes and forty lashes. There's a difference between separation and divorce. There's a difference, according to Matthew 12:31-32, between blasphemy against the Son of God and blasphemy against the Holy Spirit. There's a major difference between the works of the flesh and the fruit of the Spirit (Galatians 5). In Exodus 11:7, God even puts a difference between Egyptians and Israelites.

Staying safe on one side of a line or crossing it into danger makes all the difference. Discernment is "judging" where the line is. Seeing things as equal without distinction is critically dangerous. For the most part, the Bible shows us these lines even though the world avoids them as "divisive" and unproductive.

One day in January, my niece was showing two pigs after she had trained them for several months. I attended the show knowing nothing about pigs. I could not figure out why the judge was picking one over the other until I listened to his explanations for his choices. I then realized the importance of differences. It was no longer a gray issue of "they're all just pigs" or "they're all the same." I started to see the good and the bad, the straight backed and the curved backed. I was completely ignorant until I saw the differences. Of course the Judge knew more differences than I had learned after only one day of observation. The more a person knows about differences the more he is able to "judge" which pigs are good and which ones are bad.

I've heard that a monkey's DNA is parallel to human DNA 98% of the time, but isn't it that 2% that makes the difference? (Should we really be so gullible as to believe facial structure, stature and posture, hair patterns, and brain capability all ride on 2%?) It's really quite pitiful to see how emotional humanists get about their similarities to chimpanzees. They refuse to live with reality because they are unwilling to admit obvious discrepancies.

~~~

The Bible advises Christians to live separately from what is acceptable to the world. The world accepts evil and always will. Where there is evil, Christians are to turn away. "The fear of the Lord is to hate evil" (Prov. 8:13). Where the world is wrong, Christians are to live rightly. "What fellowship hath righteousness with unrighteousness? And what communion hath light with darkness?" (2 Cor. 6:14). Spiritual opposites should not be mixed. How can we distinguish between right and wrong or black and white if they are mixed into gray?

Ephesians 5:11 advises Christians to "have no fellowship with the unfruitful works of darkness, but rather reprove them." We are not innocent to put happy labels on pagan holidays. God spews it from his mouth (Rev. 3:15-16). He would rather we celebrate Halloween whole-heartedly as a pagan celebration than to make it a godly celebration. Will our children ever stand up to persecution if they're never denied anything? In this alone, Christians could be an example to the world if we demonstrated devotion to the Lord and hatred for evil celebrations (Ps. 97:10).

Our middle course has been that we would never pretend to be a witch or laugh at murder and mutilation on other days, but we support celebration of death on the last day in October (since the rest of the world does it too). Probably Christian tolerance for Halloween is what allowed fascination for Harry Potter and vampire sagas.

There is a balance. We don't have to be separate in things which are not immoral. For example, the world eats at Taco Bell and Christians eat at Taco Bell. The world mows their grass, we mow our grass. There are many things we do which are just like other people, probably even most things. But Christians must not ignore being separate in important things for the sake of righteousness.

All activities Christians do on a daily basis are routine, mundane, ordinary, and somewhat boring. For the most part, Christians and non-Christians act the same and live the same. So, I am not promoting riotous actions, reactions, or trouble-making in order to invoke persecution. I'm not advocating a try-to-get-noticed movement as we demand that we're different. When you consider everything a person does in a day, the part I'm writing about may be only 10% of our lives. But in a spiritual sense, it's the part that makes the difference.

Worship

Christian worship is a daily practice and a daily reflection of Christ in our lives. But for the purpose of this book, I am mainly describing worship practices inside our churches. In the Bible, worship is usually described as loud. But it does *not* mimic the loud, rebellious spirit of the world. Some church's worship is but "noise" unto the Lord (Lam. 2:7). Discernment comes from knowing the difference, not in making a "connection" to the world's music. The error of the church is in trying to sound *like* the world, implementing the latest trends into holy worship services.

Where is discernment? Where are differences? Our youth see the world has rock music and the church has rock music, the world dresses irreverently and the church dresses the same, the world has tattoos and worship leaders have tattoos, the world dances to a beat and the church dances to a beat, the world uses psychology and the church uses psychology, the world uses yoga, chanting, hypnosis, guided imagery, astral projecting, biofeedback, acupuncture, and hot stone massages to relax and some (not all) Christians do the same, the world uses certain advertising strategies to hype its products and the church does the same............. the world stresses tolerance of all creeds and the church is rapidly shifting its direction to embrace them too.

I'm not saying God does not forgive these actions. But I am saying these behaviors are, for the most part, overlooked in our churches, classified as "under the blood" and clean rather than removed as they should be. The psalmist points out how God's people are bent toward rebellion because they "were mingled among the heathen, and learned their works" (Ps. 106:35). The Lord told His people, "Ye have not walked in my statutes, neither executed my judgments, but have done after the manners of the heathen that are round about you" (Ezek. 11:12).

The paradigm shift guides this generation to follow "after the manners" of others and to use their practices to glorify God. The attitude is: "Anything goes! We are free!" Nonetheless, God rejects certain worship (See Isa. 1). Cain was not allowed to bring whatever he wanted. We rationalize, like Cain probably did, that we're not bringing a sinful thing. It's actually something we like or even our favorite thing. Cain enjoyed farming, we enjoy exercising, baking, football, painting, etc. But these are not what God has designated for worship. There's a difference in what we like and what God accepts. Ezekiel told the Israelites to go ahead and serve the idols if they chose not to listen to God, but to stop polluting His holy name with their gifts and idol worship (Ezek. 20:39). God does not appreciate His holiness mixed with our common worldliness.

We reason that we are setting something apart for God. We think it's worthy since it is not an "evil" thing. But when Saul spared the "best" of the spoils to sacrifice unto the Lord, Samuel told him he disobeyed. He said, "to obey is better than sacrifice" (1 Sam. 15:15-22). God did not want what Saul had to offer. He had already told him not to offer them. Our labels change nothing. We, like Saul, think the importance lies in our saying it is godly, not in listening to what God says about it. God is repulsed by what we've stamped with approval. (See Isa. 1.)

Labeling everything "good" has blinded us from discerning what yoga truly is........ a meditation practice used by Buddhists and Hindus. It's not "just a harmless exercise." We don't have the right to rename it when it already is what it is. The word "yoga" roughly translated is "unite" or "join" which involves "bringing the body and mind to a .... pure awareness of self without mental distractions."[8] The process does not stop there. Eastern meditation experts explain:

> There is "wholeness that occurs when the individual self.... is joined with a vision of the cosmic. Today this sense of belonging to the universe is crucial to our building a global community inclusive of all life..... The effects of yogic practice are easily verified by direct personal experience. No belief is required.[9]

Even without believing in its core intention, Christians are affected. A person cannot separate himself from something if he is right in the middle of it. We cannot justify sampling if God says to shun. The practice is said to be "the primary prerequisite to perceiving pure consciousness."[10] Pure consciousness is defined as the state of the "Spirit." Rather than claiming any relation to Christianity, yoga enthusiasts explain, "The West has always perceived God and Spirit as something separate from the world, separate from material existence" but "the East saw Spirit as consciousness, integral and intrinsic to all existence - material and nonmaterial - at every level of being. The deepest, or ultimate, plane is the realm of pure consciousness, pure spirit."[11] In other words, yoga's consciousness or Spirit or "God" is intrinsically inside everything at every level. Its goal is to "connect" with it (God). Since yoga's goal is to unite a person to the "God" present within and not to God who is separate, it cannot be compatible for Christian use. (Even when Spirit or God is capitalized, it does not necessarily mean it is the true God.)

How can we connect to God by any other means than Jesus? Jesus is the way to God, not yoga. We are outside the safety zone if we use man-made methods to gain access to God. Can a Christian reason that even though Hitler used a swastika for ungodly reasons, we'll use it as a cross in our home? A Christian may also use yoga "simply to exercise." I can almost understand the rationale. But if a person discerns that the practice and its founder (Satan) shake their fist at truth, defy God, and reject Jesus, they might rather prove loyalty to God and refuse compromise, shunning the very appearance of evil (1 Thess. 5:22).

"But they set their abominations in the house, which is called by my name, to defile it" (Jer. 32:34). Can we bring anything into the house of God (whether the temple is our body or the church) as long as we "say" we are worshiping? Does bringing it *inside* make it pure or does its presence contaminate the holy place?

~~~

Offering what God has forbidden (whether it is common or sinful) parallels the story of the young priests, Nadab and Abihu, who offered "strange fire" to God. God had already clearly specified to them how He was to be worshiped (Lev. 10:1-2). They didn't think it would make any difference. Neglect cost them their lives.

Many of the older generation question second-rate commonness in church, but the younger generation doesn't even notice its mediocrity. Chaff slips detection because those who notice have been silenced and young leaders have not been taught any difference. After being raised with crude jokes and unsuitable training in youth services, the damaged fruit feels they can worship God any way they please. Sadly, they are only doing what they've been taught. They've been taught to "come boldly before the throne" (in their flesh) rather than under the cover of Jesus' blood. They don't know about dying to fleshly desires or coming humbly before the Lord.

So, they strive to "stimulate creativity." Godly prophets called it worshiping the work of our hands (Isa. 2:8; Jer. 1:16; Acts 17:25). Ezekiel pointed out how even the ungodly Philistines were ashamed at the "lewd way" God's people were acting (Ezek. 16:27-30). Regrettably, tithes are spent on popular practices from other cultures and incorporated into worship "gatherings." Ezekiel shocked God's people with the reprimand that they were worse than a harlot because they actually paid for their idolatry rather than receiving payment to forsake God! (Ezek. 16:31-34).

God is not indifferent to our worship. There is acceptable worship and there is unacceptable worship. There are acceptable worshipers and there are unacceptable worshipers. It matters whom we worship and how we worship. (See I Kings 14:22-23; 2 Kings 17:12; Eccl. 5:1-2; Dan. 3:18; Matt.15:9; Jn. 4:21-24). Sincerity is not nearly enough. We can be sincerely wrong. As Jesus told us, we "must worship Him in spirit and in truth" (Jn. 4:24).

The Bible shows us "other" ways are unacceptable: "The prophet which shall presume to speak..... in the name of other gods..... shall die" (Deut. 18:20). Rebellion, disorder, and law-less-ness is nothing new. It is, however, becoming more prominent. The Bible told us evil would become more prevalent in the last days (1 Tim. 4:1; 2 Tim. 3:13).

Attempts to poison truth have been since the Garden of Eden. Like oil and water, poison and truth will never merge. Poison will always be poison and truth will always be truth. Knowing the difference will save lives especially when they fall under the same label. There is now more "poison" than ever, but few see it because its label reads "truth." (See 2 Thess. 2:11-12.) The alarm must be sounded as the balance *shifts* toward false and away from real. Even in our beloved Christian America, consensus is moving toward all faiths as inevitable roads to heaven.

~~~

The Old Testament's detailed description of the tabernacle and the Holy of Holies is a type for us to follow today. Even though New Testament Christians are not under ceremonial law, the purpose of the tabernacle was to exemplify the importance of preparing a place for God's presence (Ex. 25:8). God's habitation is separate/different from other places. It is a place of His choosing, not ours (See Deut. 12: 5, 11.)

The veil, which kept men out, teaches us that mankind is separated from God's holiness. Even though we now are able to enter, it did not change the fact that God remains holy. Man must become holy (through Christ) before we enter God's presence. When Christians meet inside a church, it represents a place where we meet God, a place where God is worshiped, a place which is different from the grocery store or the local mall. Christians also, personally, represent the temple. We are to treat the place of worship, whether our body or a building (whether individually or corporately), with an uncommon, reverent attitude. (I'm not advocating cold-hearted, dry Christianity. There's a difference.)

Sadly, many pastors are striving to make their churches look and feel very common just like the local coffee shop or even a movie theater. Those passing by see nothing different. We should not think the world will be drawn to the mundane. Shouldn't they see a place of respect? Instead, we create an atmosphere they pity for it's attempt to look cutting edge. Awe should be the reaction not because of the great lawn or huge edifice, but because it represents a place of dignity. It should remind them of a refuge. We should get out of the way and allow the Holy Spirit to draw people to His house.

Cold, stiff, self-righteousness has accrued valid criticism over the last few decades, but justification cannot be given to the opposite end of the spectrum....... flippancy toward God's holiness. Common is the opposite of holy. The holy places described in the Bible are "figures" of the true holy place which is heaven (Heb. 9:24). Until we are actually in heaven, we continue to have an earthly sanctuary (Acts 2:1-2). We are to respect it and recognize its representation of God to a dying world (whether it is our life or our church). It would be better for Christians not to meet publicly than to meet and abuse its meaning and significance. It would be better for a person not to claim to be a Christian than to ridicule its reputation. We should not be guilty of "casting down the dwelling place of [God's] name to the ground" (Ps. 74:7).

If God specified "holy garments" upon entering the Holy of Holies, preparation through cleansing, and demanded proper conduct inside, then shouldn't we recognize the heart of what God is saying? God has not changed (Mal.3:6).

Is Sunday Different?

New worship mimics "ritualistic practices" which may sound old-school, but actually borrow from all religions. New worship encourages us to worship any way we "feel." New thought falsely assumes God's requirements for worship are "fluid" and ever-changing because the Bible is a "living document" which "evolves" with time. (Note: The Bible truly is "living" in the sense it gives life, but not in the sense that it changes.) Claiming the world will never hear our message unless we change in order to be relevant to a declining culture, assumes God cannot speak for Himself.

"Multi-sensory worship" (alternative worship) incorporates all of the senses. Jude 19 warns of those who are "sensual, having not the Spirit." The focus of worship should be as a sweet savor unto God, not what is sweet to us. Creativity and imagination are applauded inside "gatherings" just as those activities are given high regard in Hollywood. Many are now striving to "deconstruct" and get away from organized, pre-planned, "sanity" in the church. Yes, the Holy Spirit should direct a service which may require going a different direction than planned. But change for the sake of change and disorganization for the sake of "fluidity" is not a better direction.

A casual atmosphere in the church has been something pastors have bragged about for the last few decades. It's ironic how pride in "holy" jeans and common T-shirts accuses anything different as being "arrogant." For the last two decades, we have flip-flopped down to church, then headed out to the lake to water-ski without even changing clothes. Kids are taught by our careless words and gum-chewing actions that Sunday is not set apart or different from any other day. So, naturally, an anything-goes approach to worship appeals to them.

Worship is a matter of the heart whether we are dressed up or not. It can occur anywhere as long as the person's heart is focused on God. This would discount places of ill repute unless the person is there against his will. But our actions (and clothes) do reflect the status of our heart. What does commitment look like? Job interviews are determined by clean, well-dressed, well-mannered people versus those wearing an "I don't care" attitude. It shouldn't be so touchy for Americans to admit a person's clothing really does reflect character or lack of it.

When honoring someone, at a wedding or a funeral, people try to dress respectfully. Yet, when we say we're going to meet with a holy God, our appearance shows otherwise. When we say we are honoring God, we treat church the *same* as Wal-Mart. People dress up on dates, reflecting respect rather than taking the "I really didn't give this day much thought or preparation" approach. Wearing and acting our "Sunday best" actually teaches a child respect for that day. Children should be taught the commandment to "keep the sabbath holy" is much more than lip service. (See Ex. 20:8; Lev. 19:30.)

Criticism for hypocritical Christians of the past who acted honorably and dressed up on Sunday yet were heathens the rest of the week is not to be reciprocated by lowering Sunday to a heathen day too. We fix the problem by raising the standard of the other six days. Strange how we haven't sought to reform the rest of the week while keeping Sunday set apart. Consequently, our culture is now more decadent than ever. The answers for reform lie with Christians. When God's people see the necessity to pray, humble themselves, seek God's face, and turn from their wicked ways, we'll see a difference (2 Chron. 7:14).

Since our bodies are considered the temple of God, we should be examples of Christ seven days a week. But in reference to a sabbath, it is that tithe part that should be different and set aside from our weekly routine. (Interesting note: The Bible refers to "polluting" the sabbath or "profaning" the sabbath 12 times. It's another 13 times if you include polluting the sanctuary. The Bible discusses "casting down" the sanctuary, casting "fire into" it, those who have "done wickedly" in the sanctuary, have "trodden down" or "defiled" it, and how the "heathen entered" to commit the "abomination of desolation." Along the lines of contamination, a whole book could be written on the Bible's references to polluting God's holy name.)

Do we teach our children about resting on the sabbath? It wasn't long ago secular schools wouldn't play sports on Sunday. Of course businesses stayed closed too. Without even realizing it at the time, lessons on Sunday from my parents left their mark. After first putting on a dress that morning (which my flesh never liked, but had no choice), then being told before entering the church to spit my gum into "the gum tree," then being reminded not to yell or run in the sanctuary, I realized Sunday was different. I also noticed Mom and

Dad rested that day. Any other day, my dad wore a cap and went to work, Mom was cleaning and doing laundry, and I was chewing gum, running, yelling, and wearing what I liked.

One of the answers this generation lacks is teaching on God's holiness. They need principles of consecration, dedication, and sanctification. Instead, they get a church that screams to the world, "We are just like you!" Since, we live in New Testament times, we should reflect holiness more than ever because "Of how much sorer punishment, suppose ye, shall he be thought worthy, who hath trodden under foot the Son of God, and hath counted the blood of the covenant, wherewith he was sanctified, an unholy thing, and hath done despite unto the Spirit of grace?" (Heb. 10:29).

~~~

Churches in America have had freedom to worship openly. For two centuries, their buildings have courageously upheld the name of Jesus. Christians have been free to make their pronouncement of faith public. Meetings include diverse people united by Christ. Strength comes as each person's gift is put to work in order to develop the body of Christ. Whether a toe or a knee, each person moves by the commandment (authority) of the head (Jesus). (See 1 Cor. 12:14-18). Strength has come as we have encouraged each other in our walk with God.

But there is something shocking about the new "destruction of the temple" mentality that suggests, "Wouldn't it be better if we scrapped this church thing and met in coffee houses or in people's homes?" (where everyone is sitting and equal and free to question). The early church started with a few, so it was practical they met in homes. Today it is practical to meet in larger places. Church buildings make public statements.

We must fight against the concept which desires to squelch Christianity's voice and her freedom to meet publicly. Satan wants to destroy the church's corporate strength and, eventually, the unity which is in Christ. If what has been free and out in the open becomes secret and private, each pocket will be easier to squelch. Remember the Jews hiding from the Nazis? Their freedom to be out in the open was the first step toward their elimination. We must not let the Enemy gain the upper hand by pushing the church underground.

Chapter 5

Divided Heart

> Israel ….. hath increased the altars…. Their heart
> is *divided*; now shall they be found faulty…. (Hosea
> 10:1- 2).

New Christianity worships whomever, whatever, and however it
chooses, adding to what God has established as non-negotiable. It is
the result of years of shifting and making God convenient, easy, and
according to our own schedule. We assume He follows us.

Easy access to comfort has diminished our dedication to God.
Christians' hearts are divided away from His simple, pure, perfection. As we have "waxed fat," we have forsaken God and "lightly
esteemed" the Rock of our salvation (Deut. 32). The physical realm
has distracted us from the spiritual. We obey according to what can
be seen. Both the physical and spiritual are valid in that they are real
and actually there. But humans relate to physical things more easily
because they are "sensed" and require no effort.

~~~

In the Garden of Eden, there was a tree which looked like any other
tree, but it was different, very different. It had a spiritual difference
even though it physically looked like the others. Its difference was
between life and death. Adam and Eve were to accept in faith that

it was different, trusting what God said about it. Its difference was that its fruit was to be avoided.

Today, faith to stand on what God has said is very shaky. We are told facts must be proven and only scientific evidence verifies truth. But we know by Scripture, faith itself has "substance" and its "evidence" does not come from the physical realm (Heb. 11:1). True faith is under siege because it is what gives people access to grace. (See Rom. 5:2). Grace is not received without faith.

When Adam and Eve chose to disobey, God did not consider what to do next. Instead, by His own preset law, man was instantly separated from Him. Man was banned from the garden without any valid capability of returning until God provided the answer.

Not "seeing" the devastating spiritual results of disobedience, the first humans chose to eat the fruit as Satan skillfully persuaded them. He made them rationalize that disobedience wasn't that bad. He eased Eve's fears about dying and sweetly soothed her as he cooed, "Ye shall not surely die" even after God had told her she would. Satan offered physical benefits which instantly appealed to her. He persuaded her that disobedience was "harmless" and she could even become like God. Her heart was then divided.

The first Bible story stresses the difference between obeying and disobeying God. It emphasizes the cost of disobedience that began with a divided heart. It teaches sin has consequences regardless of rule adjustments. It teaches God is serious even though we think something is harmless (or even beneficial). It teaches in spite of what we see physically, we must obey for spiritual reasons. Even though it appears the world gets away with sin, the day of regret will surely come (See Ps. 73.)

~~~

A complacent attitude toward "harmless" participation causes Christians to veer in worship. But a Christian should be able to stand before God and say, "I did not offer that which was torn, blemished, or sacrificed to idols. I did not participate in false worship. I did not agree with those who worshiped false Christs. I didn't bring you what I thought was right. I didn't do it just because everyone else did it. I drew a line of "difference between the holy and profane" (Ezek. 22).

Excuses for compromise: It's just a harmless game. It's just a cartoon. It's just a movie. It's just a story............. God made stories didn't He. God loves me no matter what. What's the big deal?"

Shadrach, Meshach, and Abednego could have reasoned: "What's wrong with bowing? I bow everyday to get things off the floor. God made us to bow or He wouldn't have given us flexible backbones." But instead, the three Hebrews knew that on that day, in that place, before that image, at that time, when the cornet sounded........... it was *wrong* to bow. Woe to those who *did* bow in allegiance and cooperation that day.

These three did not stand shamefully, with head bowed, about to collapse in fear as they faced death. No, they told the king God was able to deliver them, but even if He didn't, "be it known unto thee, O king, that we will not serve thy gods, nor worship the golden image which thou hast set up" (Dan. 3:18). "Be it known unto thee, O king." They stood with locked knees and chin up clearly showing everyone that they were *not* bowing. "Be it known," not "try to guess" what my decision is. What if they lived today? Would they say, "I'll go ahead and bow, but I'll really just tie my shoe" or "I'll go ahead and act like it, but in my heart, I'm not participating. God wouldn't want me to die because He loves me so much." American Christians avoid ridicule and being different and we aren't even facing death (yet).

The martyrs of the 16th century died because they would not compromise. The Catholic church told them communion was literally Christ's blood and body. They disagreed and would not participate. So, they died. They could have reasoned as they took communion that, "in their heart" they were not in agreement with the false interpretation. Nobody would have known the difference. But they did not choose to increase their altars by worshiping God plus their flesh's security. Instead, their action proved their loyalty to one true altar.

Our culture is clouded with so much compromise and living without clear division between Christian belief and the world's, that we don't even feel a check when crossing lines. We feel assured the Holy Spirit follows us wherever we go. To give some credit to today's mentality, most will admit bad parts of entertainment are truly bad. What we fail to admit is that those parts are affecting us, wooing us, and causing us to bow in participation. Physically, it seems the bad has no effect until, spiritually, we realize it's too late.

~~~

When addressing the churches of Asia, Jesus spoke of His hatred for the deeds of the Nicolaitans. So, Jesus actually hated something? Yes. Their anti-law mentality led to self-indulgence as they claimed their physical actions did not affect their spirit. They thought freedom from the law meant freedom to enjoy the world's attractions. Free *from* the law of sin is not freedom *to* do what we like. *There is a difference.*

When comparing physical actions of many Christians with non-Christians, there is really not much difference. Consider the speech, the interests, the entertainment, the worldly activities, etc. This is the product of Christians striving to disassociate with fundamentalism. Solving the problem of cold Christianity (not true Christianity) by swinging to the opposite end of the spectrum and shunning obedience and devotion is not the answer.

When the great harvest of the end times occurs, the tares will be separated from the wheat. (See Joel 3:13; Matt. 13:24-41; Rev. 14:15.) The non-Christians will be separated from the Christians. They look the same to us, but God knows the difference. He sees who are legitimately His (2 Tim. 2:19). Those who are not His will be "burned in the fire"(Matt. 13:40). Notice there isn't a stack of "Not Sure." There also isn't one great big stack that includes everyone. There are only two stacks separated by their differences.......... unseen, spiritual differences.

~~~

The recent predicament of Christianity is not unlike the story of the Titanic. Somebody warns about the iceberg ahead. He yells, "Turn around, we are going to hit a gigantic mountain of ice and it will take us down!" Absurdly, those playing in the band and eating their heart's fill reply, "We see the iceberg, it's not that big and your negativity is ruining our good time." Others refuse to see the iceberg. Correspondingly, the attitude is the same in our churches. "Don't tell me anything heavy, just prophecy unto me, 'Peace, peace'" (Jer. 5:31; 8:11-12; Ezek. 13:10).

The tip of the iceberg is what we physically see all around us...... a generation with major problems and churches and pastors with major weaknesses. The iceberg below the surface is the spiritual part we don't see. It is this larger, unseen part that is even more serious and detrimental than the visible surface symptoms.

We naturally want to close our eyes to "underwater" spiritual problems. Failing to admit the tip's warning is due to living by misapplied Scripture that "all things work together for good." We brush off duty and vigilance and think good will result without effort leaning toward evolutionary thinking. But with discerning eyes, the spiritual can be, in a sense, more obvious than the natural. (Side note: Christians should not make spiritual applications in every single instance. This is usually superstition or mystical fascination.) Seeing spiritually comes only through knowing God's Word. The more Scripture we know, the more we see spiritually.

Compromise Swept Under the Rug

Most movies demand physical compromise. Preachers should not be timid about stressing contradiction between them and biblical principles. Why can't we have backbone like Christians fifty years ago who considered movies to be a very serious matter? Instead those with backbone are considered too rigid. Movies are even more blatant in their profanity than fifty years ago. A Christian has only one argument in defending them: "Everyone else is doing it."

Recently, an influx of spiritual movies and television programs have flooded us with story lines promoting all religions and emphasizing "truths" from each one. Christians avoid thinking about their error. "What *difference* does it make?" The tip of the iceberg (visible) is the actual movie. The unseen mass is the effect down the road, especially for children. It's naive to think we can sail right up to the tip and avoid the underlying danger.

These programs are designed to shift Christian thinking rather than influence non-Christian viewers. It's working. Christians are now laughing and perpetuating mockery and ridicule. Paul tells us as he writes Timothy to "shun profane and vain babblings: for they will increase unto more ungodliness" (2 Tim. 2:16). Most movies and television programs advance the cancer of sin in America as they increase ungodliness. Wouldn't it impact the movie industry if Christians emphatically shunned them? Wouldn't it make a *difference* to see Christians acting and talking differently than mainstream America? Wouldn't our children reap the benefit?

Movies are definitely funny and entertaining. But entertainment should not be our priority and righteousness should be. If righteousness was our priority, we would refuse to listen to a movie *because* of its error rather than watching it *because* of its humor. Second Corinthians 7:1 tells us to "cleanse ourselves from all filthiness of the flesh and spirit, perfecting holiness in the fear of God." Proverbs 15:4 teaches a "perverse" tongue causes a "breach in the spirit."

Do Christians truly fear a breach in the spirit? Do we fear God's holiness? Do we understand how holy He is? I think it would make a difference if we did.

Satan pours the coal to his activities when he produces spiritual movies. The tip is in the titles alone. What lies beneath the surface is a huge mass ready to take the ship of Christianity to the floor of the ocean. Humans are very weak and easily succumb whenever they participate, especially in a crowd of other participants. Christians must be vigilant and uncompromising. Discernment first looks, then compares, then sees the difference. Then acts, based on that knowledge. We lack discernment because we are refusing to first look.

Faithfulness Matters

There's a reason for Christian complacency and compromise. I've listened to Christians and their responses and I've seen a pattern, a deep down belief (not necessarily wrong) that everything will work out for Christians..... a belief that as long as you go to church and say you're a Christian, you'll be safe from deception.

For instance, there's a general disagreement about the ship of Christianity going down and that faithfulness is not required to maintain Christianity's effectiveness. True, Christianity will not be snuffed out completely no matter what people do or think. God has won the victory over sin and His truth endures forever (Ps. 117:2). But Satan continually tries to hinder individual salvation. Satan's attempt to sink Christianity, and therefore truth, will be evidenced in the loss of individual souls. He wants casualties.

In America and around the world, truth is being pushed aside as this generation seeks a better way to solve global problems. But when the church leaves at the rapture, deceived individuals and their "version of truth" will be left behind. This is my concern. What do individuals really believe? Some are rejecting truth even after being raised in Christian homes, churches, and Christian schools. Individuals will be left behind to stand against popular opinion in order to save their souls, yet standing with popularity is what left them there!

Proverbs 10:30 states the "the righteous shall never be removed." So, a remnant is definitely safe and most Christians believe they are that remnant. But my concern is for those who just miss it as they pursue popular "truth" and listen to glossy imitations offered from postmodern pulpits and Christian bookstores. Christians are vulnerable in their carelessness. Parents may be saved and going to heaven, but their vigilance and guardianship for their child's soul has been insufficient.

Following trends (even Christian trends) follows security. "Christian" children do not gain heaven because their colorful youth group gave them chill bumps in the form of bizarre mysticism. Nor as recent shifts have preached, do they enter heaven by acts of human justice. We can't presumptuously assume we can't be deceived just because "that's not God's will."

Christian upbringing is the best and safest way to raise a child. Christian homes, generally, produce Christian children. However, today's church ironically lessens the odds for godly offspring because of current deception. Raised with a distorted view of truth only makes it harder to accept real truth because error must first be erased. In a postmodern world, the church is producing a generation of hybrids rather than a godly seed.

Inclusive blanket-salvation theology is perpetuated as mega churches resist offending their flock. One worship leader at a well-known church in Texas is quoted in a popular Christian magazine, "The only way for our worship to truly be pure is for us to receive His pure love for us. We must realize that no matter what, He loves us."[1] Here again, this generation gets the signal from church leaders that we *only* need accept God's love in order to be pure. Jesus is the "author of eternal salvation unto all them that *obey* him" (Heb. 5:9). Where is obedience if we only accept love? Where's repentance? The cost of the cross is unknown to many under age thirty. Is the belief that God loves them "no matter what" the reason they pursue worldliness?

So, Judas, Hitler, Pol Pot, Gandhi, Bin Laden, and Muhammad made it to heaven because "no matter what" God loved them? This would be the natural deduction of today's youth since they have not been taught otherwise...... that God has made his love *available* to men "no matter what," but if a person refuses His love, refuses to acknowledge and obey His commandments, and rejects His Son, he goes to hell............. "no matter what" (a place separated from His love).

I'm Really First

Lately, there are two opposite approaches concerning salvation. Some question if every one really goes to heaven because of "new truth" (like me) and others question salvation through "old-time religion." This Sunday your preacher may question who is going to heaven, but discern if he is doubting those who embrace all views or if he is doubting those who adhere to only one way. *There is a difference* and both are occurring.

Some Christians contentedly think if their child walks into a church building for more activities than the average child, he automatically goes to heaven in the end. They *trust* what is going on inside even though it is rare for the young teacher to know much of God's Word. They feel their child is getting top-notch spiritual guidance as videos of celebrities are praised. The rambling celebrity emphasizes his sinful past, says God loves him, then ends with a simple phrase, "I am second." After five minutes in the limelight, it is a bit of a stretch to think he actually believes he is second. What about teaching a child to be last, putting others second, and God first? What about a video where a person talks about God (not himself) for 5 minutes, then says, "God is first"? The impact would be different.

We must think realistically. Are our children listening to social media more hours than they spend time with God? Are they even hearing God's Word while in church as their youth pastor condemns previous views of truth and waves a candy-coated doctrine of peace? I'm afraid many parents have abdicated their duty to teach their children as they pass the job off to an impotent youth ministry.

Talking to His people in 2 Chronicles 36, God said He "sent to them by His messengers (prophets).... but they mocked the messengers of God, and despised His words .... until there was no remedy" (vs.15-16). Jeremiah tells us God commanded *His people* (not the world) to "obey.... but they hearkened not..... and went backward, and not forward" (Jer. 7: 24). Verse 26 tells us they "hardened their neck: they did worse than their fathers." If a person resists God's warning to be separate, he being "often reproved hardeneth his neck, shall suddenly be destroyed, and that without remedy" (Prov. 29:1).

Christians can no longer believe, "it won't happen to me and my church family because I love God." The people of God in the il-lustration above would not have denied their love for God. They were His people. But obedience was lacking. Proof of their love was lacking. They honored Him with their lips, but their heart was far from Him (Matt. 15:8). God's people can be deceived if they ignore extreme vigilance for the enemy's tactics. It requires knowing His Word and seeing with spiritual eyes the spiritual battle for this generation. If a person is unaware of the battle, he becomes a casualty. Christians who make it to heaven because of foundational truth, may be racked with grief to look down into hell and see their children's terror-stricken eyes pleading, "Why didn't you teach me the seriousness of obedience?" (See Isa. 17:11.)

As our hearts are divided, our mouths say God is first, but our actions say the world's viral information is first. We "profess that [we] know God; but in works [we] deny Him" (Titus 1:16). We have the works of social justice down, yes, but not dying to the flesh and being separate from the world. In that area of obedience, we are distracted by the world, letting it have free reign of our time. We speak its language without rebuke in our homes, letting it sear our conscience by degrees. We are listening to many voices and God's is just one in the mix. We forget that hearing Him requires quietness and undivided attention.

~~~

Lot was the "righteous" person in the story of Sodom and Gomorrah, but Scripture informs us that he "vexed his righteous soul with their unlawful deeds" in "seeing and hearing" (2 Pet. 2:8). It all started when he pitched his tent *toward* Sodom (Gen. 13:12). It all started when he ignored the visible tip of the iceberg. "Seeing and hearing" is exactly what vexes our souls as we sit in front of the TV, inside movie theaters, or listen to social media. It affects our thoughts and eventually our actions. It certainly affects our conscience as we become more and more calloused.

Compromise starts small then grows. Its increments aren't easily detected. But all the while, it leads us down the road to deception without "remedy" (2 Chron. 3:15-16). Compromise is another name for the "shift" in the paradigm. It's sad to think how many people will end up in hell thinking, "How in the world did I get here? I said I believed in Jesus!" But Jesus was just one of many. He believed Jesus, but didn't reject others.

That person believes a new definition of salvation which requires only accepting Jesus' love. He worships "love" rather than Jesus. He "loves" other things as much as he loves Jesus. His focus is in joining tribes of men, not joining men to God. He doesn't adhere to the exclusivity of Jesus. Compromise with other belief systems proves he is not devoted to God.

Christians aren't familiar with what "holy" and "pure" really mean. Physically, people want to drink pure water without contaminants. We resolve to eat organic foods without chemicals and we are adamant about products without fillers and additives. But spiritually, we allow contamination and pollution. We follow the broad majority rather than God's narrow truth. (Interesting note: under "contaminate" in the thesaurus is the word "adulterate.")[2]

The gospel points to genuine heart change when someone becomes a Christian. God is concerned with inward religion, which takes care of outward religion and, thus, physical compromise. Many of God's commandments require outward action to prove the heart is willing to obey. A Christian cannot say one thing and do another. He cannot say he is different when he is not.

Our culture has been in a slow boil as we fail to be shocked at boldness and vulgarity. We feel we would never "agree" with what is spoken in movie theaters. But paying money, listening, laughing, and quoting, is in fact reconciliation with evil into a life that should be holy. (See Isa. 55:2.) "How shall I pardon thee for this? Thy children have forsaken me, and sworn by them that are no gods: when I fed them to the full, they then committed adultery, and assembled themselves by troops in the harlots' houses" (Jer. 5:7).

It is counting Jesus' blood as unholy to participate and agree with wrongdoing (See Heb. 10:29.) When we show no disagreement, we show agreement. We should be repulsed by most of the entertainment offered today. These things should not entice a changed, undivided heart. We should refuse them for their indecency. We should refuse them for their blasphemy. We should refuse them for their distraction from holiness no matter how small the part may seem.

We participate because of a "new morality".... we don't want to be judgmental. Sometimes, we're just curious or just want to see what everybody is talking about. Eve was curious. Satan snorts a laugh and kindly suggests, "Did God say this would vex your righteous soul? Just look and listen. It won't hurt anything."

~~~

Why is there no difference between us and them? "New morality" tells us "them" is a 4-letter word. The world would rather the term "us" be used when referring to "others" because of our human connection. "Them" is a discriminating term. "Them" implies separation.

The spiritual reason "us and them" is not tolerated is because it is the language of the Bible. The divisive language of the Bible is under criticism in a world moving toward unified globalism. The Bible offends the world's mindset. Christians now compromise because the new way *really* sounds more loving and right.

> For the preaching of the cross is to THEM that perish foolishness; but unto US which are saved it is the power of God (1 Cor. 1:18). (See also: Ex. 11:7; Ezek. 7:11; Matt. 13:38; 1 Jn. 3:10).

Could using that "language" alone be the instigator for persecution?

There are no differences between people *with* Jesus' blood. (Acts 15:8-9; See also Rom.3:22). It is in Jesus we find true unity. Everybody, no matter their race, age, or ability, can be united in Christ. He (not love) is the unifying principle and the hope for mankind. Jesus is the primary source of unity while love is a benefit and secondary result.

Love is a definite attribute of God. His love is pure and perfect. The Bible tells us to keep ourselves "in the love of God" (Jude 21). But love itself can be misplaced or misapplied. People can love the wrong things. (See Prov. 8:36; Jer. 5:31; Matt. 6:5, 23:6; 1 Jn. 2:15.) There are other "loves" we must avoid because of their perversion. All love is not equal. We must see their differences. God is love, but love is not God.

When tempted to compromise, our immediate reaction is to smear the line until it is grayed with "does it really matter?" Lately, we have departed so far from drawing a clear line that gray is our most comfortable zone. Isn't it hard to draw a line we would never cross even to the point of death? Society has made it distasteful and uncomfortable to choose sides. Peace with others seems the most righteous thing we can do. We are quick to move the line in order to keep peace and avoid hurting feelings..... or being rejected. Any criticism for Hollywood is met with, "Can't you overlook that stuff?" A Christian immediately apologizes for offending his friends. Satan is clever to back us into a corner with the decision to either stick to our guns (and be "judgmental") or give in for the sake of peace.

Catering to the physical realm and walking by sight gives Hollywood an advantage. Music designed to affect emotions, extreme drama, high-tech action, and computerized effects impact our flesh. They are very, very persuasive as the story builds and the timing makes us actually feel the character's emotions. They know just when to emphasize and just how to zoom in on certain facial expressions to drive home the new perspective of right and wrong. Reading the Bible, which has no dramatic effects, comes across as a real low having only words written on a page. Sadly, many in hell regret how they had searched and searched for truth only to have had it discreetly gathering dust on a shelf right beside their televisions.

As church priorities shift toward global cooperation, we must realize God trumps relationship, community, and even family (Matt. 19:29). As society falls lower and lower, our standard cannot go with it to appease our conscience when we put "family first" or care for the physical needs of others. Yes, these are a step up from our current culture, but they are still a far cry from the answers we seek. It is only our reasonable duty to have a godly family and feed the poor. Putting people first falls short of putting God first.

Part 2

The Difference Between Christianity and Other Religions

Chapter 6

Spiritual Eyes

Dissenting Voices

The more a person hears a particular voice, the more easily he recognizes it. In the same sense, the more we spend time with God, the more we know His voice. There are many voices (spirits) and only one is the right one. It matters what voice we listen to and what ones we resist. Heeding voices without discrepancy is dangerous.

More often than not, voices or sudden thoughts are from the world, Satan, or our flesh. How can a person make distinctions when unsure of the source? The answer is somewhat simple, but acquisition takes time. God's voice is known by agreement with His Word. The better we know His Word, the better we know His voice. The more we know, the more easily and instantly we detect misfits.

It's when we seek Him that we find Him. He doesn't just sneak up and deposit truth if we are doing our own thing. Unsaved people do not get saved if they seek truth in the wrong places. I once was looking for my keys in my purse. I looked and looked, but they were not there. They were in my pocket. In the same way, the "key" to eternal life is not anywhere but where it truly is. It can't be found in other places even if a person truly believes it's there. "Salvation is far from the wicked: for they seek not *thy* statutes"(Ps. 119:155). A person only finds God when he finds *His* statutes and agrees with what is written in God's Word.

If we hear something that agrees with God's Word, then we know it's Him. But it's not always that simple. Sometimes Satan uses a scripture, but with a twist as he adds, takes away, or misapplies. Isaiah speaks of people who mention God, but not in truth or in righteousness (Isa. 48:1). There are also those who "are unlearned and unstable [who] wrest …. the scriptures unto their own destruction" (2 Pet. 3:16). So, we really, really need to know God's Word to catch unsound doctrine.

Intensified efforts to move all religions toward unity has only accelerated and reinforced deception. Those among our "own selves" are "speaking perverse things, to draw away disciples after them" and urge Christianity to join the global family (Acts 20:29-30). The Bible is quoted in any way, in any context, to prove any point. When the context is unknown to the hearer, he readily accepts it, assuming it is true since it came from the Bible.

Jesus said in John 10:27, "My sheep hear my voice, and I know them, and they follow me." The hearing part is very important. It would be very disheartening to think you heard God, then find out you followed another voice. A person doesn't just luck out and follow Jesus by accident or because he "meant" to do the right thing. He especially doesn't succeed just because he got into a group who thought they were hearing God. Good intentions aren't validated by the Bible. Sincerity is discounted if it's misdirected.

We cannot say that anything classifies as God's voice. Our thoughts in a journal most of the time are simply thoughts in a journal. Dreams, for the most part, are results of normal brain activity. Superstition or an "it was meant to be" attitude only adds to complacency which neglects to find out what God is really saying.

Ezekiel warns how leaders, like wolves out for dishonest gain, devise lies and say, "Thus saith the Lord God, when the Lord hath not spoken" (Ezek. 22:28). Malachi wrote, "Ye have wearied the Lord with your words. Yet ye say, wherein have we wearied him?" The answer: "When ye say, Every one that doeth evil is good in the sight of the Lord, and he delighted in them; or, Where is the God of judgment?" (Mal. 2:17). By reading this verse slowly, we see how today we justify tolerance in the same way. New Christianity teaches that God delights in everything and would never judge anyone.

The new gospel supposes God is pleased with everyone "no matter what" and only winks at sin. We now have the perspective that a person is hurting (rather than rebelling). Other slants say that since we all have a sin nature, we needn't worry because God expects us to mess up or He doesn't require obedience because it's just too hard. Television doesn't help as it bombards us with the idea that no human appetite can be controlled. God is weary of our hollow response, "What am I doing wrong?" It's like a rebel who looks up in the middle of his lawlessness with his palms toward the ceiling and says, "What?" There is no fear of God in that response.

~~~

Satan will never completely win the war. But he will gain souls of those who cooperate. He's been calculating and perfecting his methods for centuries. He persuasively mixes scriptures with lies, flips meanings, and applies references to Jesus/His kingdom to himself/his kingdom. The loophole will only be seen by its disagreement with Scripture as a whole. We must, "by reason of use have [our] senses exercised to discern *both* good and evil" (Heb. 5:14). Remember, exercise is a continual action that may even make our spiritual muscles ache.

Discernment between right and wrong must be our priority or the tide of "oneness," painted with a colorful brush of unity, peace, and love, will sweep away the average uncommitted "Christian". The difference between Christianity and other world religions is as noticeable as the opposites of left/right, up/down, north/south. But it is obvious only to spiritual eyes. There is a great gulf fixed between good and evil, between heaven and hell, and between Christianity and other religions.

"The natural man receiveth not the things of the Spirit of God: for they are foolishness unto him: neither can he know them, because they are spiritually discerned" (1 Cor. 2:14). When the disciples asked Jesus the sign of the end of the world, Jesus answered, "Take heed that no man deceive you." He went on to say "many" would be deceived as others came in His name and claimed to be the real Christ (or even the "spirit" of Christ). (Matt. 24:3-5).

Notice "many" will be deceived. If a person does not walk with his spiritual eyes open, he's headed toward deception. Even though God's way is foolishness to popular consensus and mass media, it is the way Christians must follow. It is clear as Jesus continued teaching His disciples in this Olivet discourse that, as a result of deception, not all people will end up in heaven. Matthew 25:31-46 records Jesus' words saying:

> When the Son of Man shall come..... before Him shall be gathered all nations: and He shall separate them one from another.... and He shall set the sheep on His right hand, but the goats on the left. Then shall the King say unto them on His right hand, Come, ye blessed of my Father, inherit the kingdom.... Then shall He say also unto them on the left hand, Depart from me, ye cursed, into everlasting fire.... And these shall go away into everlasting punishment: but the righteous into life eternal. (See also Rom. 9:22; 1 Pet. 2:7-8.)

Very divisive language.

Are People Different?

Jesus' words are hard to swallow because we live in a world where we walk by sight. It is so much easier to see the outside -- that everyone is the same (physically) as they live out their "story." But spiritually, there are two types of people. We cannot ignore the principle of sheep and goats.

All people are alike and equal (at birth). Luke points this out in the book of Acts. God made of "one blood all nations of men" (Acts 17:26). We listen to society's emphasis on connection because we see that everyone truly has a different story and, in a way, the same story, one that is common to all. Society is not wrong to point out physical similarities. But it is wrong to eliminate spiritual differences when they are imperative to real life.

~~~

Mass media appears to acknowledge differences as it "celebrates diversity," but this is not focused on differences at all. The intent is to unite, ultimately leading to spiritual differences merging and being equal, not being separate and unequal. "Celebration of diversity" borrows a Christian principle but distorts it. The true church represents a place where each Christian's separate gifting is used to benefit the whole body of Christ. The true application of celebrating diversity requires all members to obey one truth (the head) who is Jesus. The distortion is when the "diversity" falls under any head or leadership. All "leaders" receiving equal recognition eliminates submission to one true leader. It's a freakish concept with many heads. (See Rev. 13:1.)

So, the real connection and real application of celebrating diversity is when considering three brothers (in the Lord). One may be from Asia, one from Germany, and another from a country in Africa. They are all Christian, diverse, yet the same in Christ. On the other hand, if these three are different in their religion, they cannot be connected or celebrated. Never will public media "celebrate diversity" by opening the floor for disagreement where the rubber meets the road. New democracy allows only consenting voices, not dissenting voices. It is therefore, mob rule.

When Christians see the tide swinging in favor of gay marriage, abortion, other religions, etc., we must disagree. If society praises new freedoms that include women, blacks, Latinos, Asians, lesbians, and gays, we must see how right it is to include the first four and how wrong to include the second two (an example of "listing" which includes misfits).

So, all men are alike physically. [Exception: God chose Israel as a "special people .... above all people that are upon the face of the earth" (Deut. 7:6; Ex. 19:5). Sometimes we Christians fail to remember that even the New Covenant was originally given to Israel. (See Jer. 31:31-34; Heb. 8:8-12.)]. It is the *spirit* of a man that makes him different. As the passage from Matthew read earlier, there is only one division with two sides. To admit there are two kinds of people is a very hot spot. It is "hate talk". But real hate is in thinking everyone is alike (spiritually).

The Spirit Realm is Never Neutral

This book would be too thick if I included all the differences mentioned in Scripture between the right spirit and the wrong spirit. So, suffice it to say when something is spiritual, it is either right or wrong according to God. The spirit realm is never neutral.

Note: If something is of the wrong spirit, there are *no* differences between it and something else of the wrong spirit. Deuteronomy 18 lists several activities associated with the wrong spirit. Whether it be horoscopes, wizards, necromancy, eastern meditation, telepathy, ESP, black magic, white magic, or even Disney magic, there is *no* difference in their origin.

When comparing wrong spirits with the right spirit, there are major differences. The new spirituality, and its clever approach, is now trying to make all things (whether of the right spirit or the wrong spirit) rooted into "One" spirit. All things spiritual are now categorized simply as "spiritual" or "supernatural" without distinction.

They are said to emanate from the same "Source" of truth ("God") or from a "Universal Spirit."

Inside Christianity, vigilance is low. Careless compromise has allowed other worship practices, other rituals, sensual manifestations, and quotations from other texts to stake a claim in our church services. Another spirit has come right into God's house, joining itself with Christianity. Simplicity labels it all the same.

On prime time television, a "valid" doctor claimed that ESP is the "real sixth sense." A 20/20 episode devoted a whole hour to the sixth sense conjuring respect for communicating with the dead. Past Christians knew extrasensory perception was the wrong spirit. (ESP is not the same as when God speaks to prophets.) Christians should not be persuaded no matter how much the audience cheers invalid conclusions. Sadly, we are easily influenced if a doctor states "research shows" or "studies have proven."

There is definitely spiritual hunger in America and Satan will not passively sit by or procrastinate if there's opportunity to deceive. Twenty years ago, Christians pushed aside spiritual things with disinterest. Satan jumped in to fill the spiritual void with material interests: "Seven ways to fix your life," "Six ways to be happy," "Five ways to get rich." We ran to seminars as we tried to give substance to anything superficial. Like Israel who vomited back the quail, we are now sick of so much physical gluttony.

Now we hunger for spiritual things and Satan has his spoon ready. He presents a tasty dish of loving tolerance and even self-sacrifice to help the plight of mankind. Correcting society's problems and setting up our own kingdom pushes eternal life to the back of our mindset as we only see the need to cure visible devastation and physical death in the world. Sadly, we label a physical cure as a spiritual endeavor.

Jesus' command to "feed my sheep" is spiritual in that people need the gospel. He is the Bread of Life which satisfies man's hunger. (See

Jn. 6:35, 51.) The only thing that quenches the world-wide thirst for truth is the Living Water. Jesus said, "Whosoever drinketh of the water that I shall give him shall never thirst" (Jn. 4:14).

~~~

Spiritually, there are people who are alive and then there are walking dead men. There's a big difference. There may be dead men in churches who are only stuffed with physical things and there may be men, outside churches, who are spiritually alive. God knows for sure who are His. A parent's job is to be vigilant and know when his child's youth pastor is merely feeding young minds with physical interests. He also should make sure that if in fact the pastor is spiritually-minded, the right spirit is taught. If the pastor's motive is actually to seek souls and not just bodies, it should be to save them not deceive them.

You'll find on church websites many youth pastors' interests are only centered on the world. Holiness is the furthest thing from their minds. Quoting lyrics from secular music, secular literature, television programs, and unholy movies reveal their lack of time spent with God's Word. Their *spiritual* appetite, according to their own admission, is filled with the latest books on witchcraft and sorcery. These websites are red flag indicators of what youth groups are teaching....... more of what society and culture offer (See Matt. 12:34).

Some youth pastors show sympathy for other religions as they list what "fascinates" them. Christian issues are not listed. Biblical vocabulary is missing. Human issues are prevalent. Grasping after the very things highly promoted in our corrupt culture, they listen to their digital device and promote stories, art, ideas, people, culture, and of course "deep conversations" with all perspectives. Adversely, public media is what fills the day of those who should be seeking God. How refreshing to find a youth pastor whose electronic device is off and his Bible open.

After reading several books, I've noticed how many Christian authors live by the motto: "Let technology be your guide." It's a sign of current spiritual starvation to recognize that many (not all) believe a smart phone is really smart. Some may even think the GPS can lead them to heaven.

In recent years, the world's quest for spirituality without God has plunged our young people into a serious dilemma. We must discern if our pastors are truly involved in the *right* spirit and not with "signs and lying wonders" of the "new spirituality" currently rolling out the red carpet to usher in its emerging leader. (See 2 Thess. 2:9.)

The paradigm is shifting and children (raised in church) are rejecting once-preached, well-defined truth. They are disgusted with anything "dogmatic" and against the flow of humanity's (social media's) goal of peace and consensus. I once heard a wise woman (my mom) say, "The bad thing about young people is they believe what they hear. However, the good thing about young people is they believe what they hear." We must reach this generation with truth while there is still time!

~~~

"Positive tolerance" stresses we affirm those with whom we disagree. To affirm someone's statement means to place their belief as positive and not negative. Affirming a statement also gives it a measure of validity. Sure, Satan wants us to affirm everything. First he wants error spoken, then he wants it accepted. However, spiritual statements of the wrong spirit must be refuted. How cruel to affirm and agree with statements that ultimately lead a person to eternal pain and anguish. Is that positive?

Sometimes we cannot instantly refute lies because it will only cause a rebellious reaction and a hardened heart. Rebuttals do not apply to all cases. Sometimes, we need to listen and, over time, turn thinking toward the truth of the Bible. Guidance from the Holy

Spirit will help us know how to handle each situation wisely. But we must *always* strive to lead others toward truth and not affirm lies, especially in our own households. If Americans continue to agree and participate with the spirit of the age, error will gain the upper hand. Eventually, a tsunami will sweep away truth and its adherents, making persecution commonplace in a land once called a "nation under God."

A life-on-the-surface mentality as we run from movie to theme park to buy whatever we see advertised, tweeting, blogging, facebooking, etc. has benefited Satan as he causes people to forfeit their responsibility to consider consequences. Young people, and many parents, are being indoctrinated by very shallow sources. Even Christians meet and discuss the latest without ever mentioning something of substance.

Where is our heart? Do we impatiently look at our watches in the movie theater so we can return home to pick up where we left off in our Bible reading? Do we ever leave because what is shown is so shallow and worthless we don't have time for it? Where's the refuting, resisting, and reproving (Eph. 5:11)?

In recent years, wrong statements are not even considered to be wrong. Lies go right over our heads every day. I can safely say if a person listens to more than one hour of social media per day, he has heard at least one lie. Do Christians recognize them, then reject them in their homes? To teach discernment, family members could discuss all the lies they heard that day (a lie is anything that is not true). Parents might be shocked by this exercise when they see how difficult it is for their children to admit something is a lie.

~~~

Even as the church has misdirected her interests, God is nonetheless "longsuffering to us-ward, not willing that any should perish" (2 Pet. 3:9). Concerning other religions and their rejection of God, the prophet Ezekiel tells us God has "no pleasure in the death of the wicked: but that the wicked turn from his way and live" (Ezek. 18:23; 33:11). Our job as Christians is to turn our interest toward God, seek our fulfillment in Him, then point others to the life that is in Christ.

Chapter 7

How the Paradigm Shifted

Remember a paradigm is a system, a pattern, or a way of doing things. Since the early church of Paul's day, the Christians' pattern for living has been based on the Bible. The current shift is to abandon "dogmatic" principles in God's Word and turn toward an open-minded version. We first shifted as we tolerated any version of the Bible allowing anybody the opportunity to add, revise, eliminate, or write his own perspective. (It is unwise to change what has been changed and then change it again. Like modern dictionaries, revision has only watered down real meanings. Most of the original may still be there, but it is lacking in fundamental substance. Plus, memorization occurs best when verses are stated the same way every time. The main reason I'm compelled to defend the older version is to balance the fierce criticism against it. Oddly, Christians are now ashamed to be affiliated with it. Satan criticizes foundations in order to eliminate them.)

How has the church shifted from certainty toward flirting with other belief systems? We have cowered to criticism and finger-pointing accusations. We have knelt to allegations of a "closed mind." We don't want to seem "ignorant" or "unwilling to be challenged" by other possibilities. We have caved to charges that we fear "discovering something new" and that we should erase our "preconceived ideas." Coercion has buckled our defenses.

The colossal feat of shifting even solid Christianity toward counter-truth has not been accomplished overnight. It has been gradual, but steady. If Satan must have a virtue, it's patience. Years of complacency and diminished love for the truth has caused us to walk by sight, ignoring the spiritual tide sweeping souls of this generation to their death. We have disobeyed God's warning to seek not "after your own heart" and have, instead, devised new ways of conducting Christianity. (See Num. 15:39; Deut. 11:16; 29:18; 1 Kgs. 12:29-33).

Even the Elect

Revised Christianity, relevant for our culture, has turned our attention away from God's way and shifted allegiance toward man's way. The shifting paradigm is evidenced as creeds, songs, and phrases heard inside contemporary churches fit both Christianity AND humanism. Application can be made to both extremes through use of indirect vocabulary. The older generation is not offended by new language since the words do, although indirectly, apply to Christianity. "He" or "You" or "the One" instead of proper names for God don't prick older mindsets because, knowing what they know, they direct their singing to the God of the Bible.

On the other hand, the younger generation sees a connection based on what they know. The indirect phrases align with what they hear in their digital world. Songs about "Him" and His love and power fit their perspective, too. Their view yearns for a hero who will solve the world's problems....... some humanitarian who will join all nations as "the One" who eradicates war and solves the plight of overthrown governments and poor economies. To young people in church, "He" receives their praise, not necessarily Jesus of the Bible. Since they are not receiving information that discredits what they hear in the world, the new phrases (in church) are actually indoctrinating them further to receive the Antichrist. Sadly, older Christians are not picking up on the shift. It is a very clever maneuver of an Enemy who has every intention of misleading.

New songs are deficient of specific biblical language and facts about "Him" (Jesus). When Bible memorization has faded from an older generation's memory and, as a result, has not even been passed to the next, the field becomes ripe for new doctrine where only the label is biblical. Lack of biblical terms in new music is not recognized when it was never taught in the first place. We think surely our children are singing about God and worshiping Him. Surely they would never think some handsome movie star or government leader could solve the Earth's problems.

New worship lyrics are very vague, general, and without distinction. Many youth are singing to God, but in many cases, their words focus on man rather than God. "I would give my life to live for everything I believe in" registers with a believer of truth, but also hits home with a believer of whatever he wants to call truth. According to this song, it's the belief that matters, not *what* you believe. Tragically, this is how a contemporary song in our church works for the older generation, but also meets with a younger person's view of truth. A person who gives his life to live for whatever promises a better world, readily extends a hand in agreement to receive an implanted mark of unity.

When youth sing "Christ is enough for me" or "Everything I need is in you" they believe nothing is required of them. Older people see the depth of these words based on the whole of Scripture, not a literal interpretation. The paradigm shift has cleverly eliminated instruction about covenant bond and the requirements of those who agree to it. To this generation, the "all" in "Jesus Paid It All" means God requires no duty, no loyalty, no obedience.

Missiles land in our churches because pastors have not been vigilant in protecting their flock. Ezekiel speaks of God's people becoming "meat to all the beasts of the field, because there was no shepherd" (Ezek. 34:8). Literally, Satan is devouring sheep with his "sacred romance." Christians tend to think they cannot be deceived because they just "know" when something is error. We cannot "know" right from wrong unless we implant truth from an outside source. An applicable verse must already be in our spirit to "know" if something is right or wrong. Since Satan attacks from all angles, each angle must be covered by Scripture. It takes different scriptures for different attacks. Many believe they will "feel" when something is wrong or deceptive. True, if a person's feelings are sensitive to God's Word. But feelings sensitive to the world and walking by sight are easily misled. Satan relies on the weakness of self-trust in Christians and seeks to deceive even the elect. Paul told the Corinthians, "Let him that thinketh he standeth take heed lest he fall" (1 Cor. 10:12).

Ezekiel also slaps God's people with reality when he says we have been sacrificing our sons and daughters with whoredoms (Ezek. 16:20). Flirting with the world leads our children into adultery with the world's beliefs. By acknowledging beliefs contrary to truth, the church is not only unfaithful to her husband, Jesus, but is sacrificing her young people to the gods of this world.

We have obscured truth as we avoid cut and dried statements. Without proper training and specific direction, children automatically put labels of truth on anything. We should be praying for Christians to give their lives for truth (not merely for their belief). We must make clear to this generation that truth is the only thing worthy of dedication and its only source is the Holy Bible of Christianity.

~~~

Another shift in teaching is when the "first" commandment (to love God with our whole heart) and the "second" commandment (to love men) are considered equal commandments. Their difference, simply put, is first comes before second. God makes it clear in the Bible that He is first and nothing is *beside* Him in rank or position. Loving our neighbor comes second to loving God. Actually, brotherly love is contingent on loving God.

The new way advocates putting man equal to God. It pushes a doctrine of a "flattened world" without authority and without hierarchy.

It promotes loving our fellow man as priority, preaching it as the "true gospel" that will save the world. The church continues to shift as she refuses to remain separate in her doctrine, putting God above man. Satan has even convinced us that certain fundamental truths are actually "wrong." We now find ourselves in a hot front-line battle for what is left of truth in the church. Satan's advantage is the zealous nature of young people who have the passion to defend what the world calls truth and oppose what it calls divisive.

~~~

Satan has shamelessly shifted the paradigm in several areas. He feeds us appetizer lies before he brings out the big turkey. He knows that nobody in church will automatically swallow the big one (that Jesus is found in all religions) until we compromise by agreeing all religions have a certain "element" of truth.

Even if other religions have "Jesus" in their writings, he is not the son of God, he is not able to save from sin, and he's simply a teacher or a prophet. "He" is not the Jesus of the Bible. We cannot say Jesus is in all religions, because they do not profess the true Jesus. The real Jesus has specific, narrow, authentic qualities........... found only in the Bible. (Mentioning Jesus in other texts can spark interest for the true Jesus.)

The actual shift involves turning away from truth and turning toward a lie. (See 2 Tim. 4:4; Jer. 2:13.) It's what Jeremiah called forsaking God, the fountain of living waters, and hewing out broken cisterns that can hold no water (Jer. 2:13; also Jdgs. 2:13). Turning (forsaking) may take years and those affected don't even notice the deviations.

God is Everywhere, But Not in Everything

> The eyes of the Lord are in every place, beholding the evil and the good (Prov. 15:3).

Satan plants side-tracking lies. They are somewhat out of step with truth rather than blatant in their nature. They sound harmless, but do veritable damage when applied as he intends. They're kinda true or even half-true. They are either worldly doctrines mixed with biblical doctrines or outright false applications to truth.

For example, we hear "life is in all matter" or there is "energy" in all matter. It sounds true enough, scientifically, if you consider cell movement as energy though this movement is not necessarily life. Many who promote evolution see water as a sign of life since they think the first creature crawled out of it. Heat waves from a fire are not "alive" even though they generate motion. But aside from science, this energy many times is even referred to as "spirit." New Agers and Oprah-ites use "energy" when referring to "God." The culmination of this error claims this energy/spirit/God is the same and is in all matter.

But *there is a difference.* Energy is not God and God is not energy. Energy is only something created. God is a Spirit, but that Spirit is not "energy" nor was His Spirit created (Jn. 4:24). On one side, there are evil spirits, lying spirits, perverse spirits, and unclean spirits (1 Sam. 16:23; 2 Chron. 18:21; Isa. 19:14; Matt. 12:43). These are created. On the other extreme, there is the Holy Spirit who was never created.

In the category of created spirits, there is the spirit of man and the spirit of animals. These are different spirits. (See Eccl. 3:21). Animals are not equal to humans (Gen. 1:26). Some animals, like frogs, represent unclean spirits (Rev. 16:13). There is a difference between animals and trees because trees have no spirit. Key: All things do not have the same spirit even though they were all created *by* the same Spirit.

The spirit inside man is not the same as the Spirit of God. God's Spirit bears witness *with* a Christian's spirit that we are the children of God (Rom. 8:16). His Spirit can be *in* us or *on* us, but our spirit never becomes God's Spirit. He renews our spirit, but it does not actually change into His Spirit. We are unified with His Spirit, but our spirit remains separate from His Spirit. In other words, we will never be God.

Christians compromise (big time) when they agree that all spirits are the same and are, therefore, the spirit of God. Even though God created all things, He is not *in* all things...... or *in* all matter...... or *in* all religions..... or in *all* people. How could Satan be God? God is truth and there is no truth in Satan (Jn. 8:44). So, we must apply the brakes back at the root and disagree by saying, "God is not *in* all matter."

There is a difference between the "children of God" (because He created all men) and actually being a "child of God" based on conversion from our original father (the devil) to another Father (God). Belief in human divinity is found with statements like "we must be our real self" or "find our true self" indicating mankind is holy at its root. New spirituality persuades us to rely on humanity's goodness as the cornerstone tenet for achieving world peace. But it is God and not us, who changes the world. He must increase, we must decrease (Jn. 3:30).

Man Naturally Does Wrong

Even though the majority is quickly accumulating proponents toward believing all things contain God's essence, spirit, or energy or that all belief systems contain an element of truth, the majority is wrong. *There is a difference* between truth and other views no matter the appearance. Truth is determined by its validity. Truth is based in God's Word, not man's word. In these last days, to avoid being deceived, WE MUST KNOW GOD'S WORD to know differences between truth and lies. (Notice truth is singular and lies are plural.) Elijah withstood 450 prophets of Baal. Elijah was right and 450 were wrong. (See I Kgs. 18:25.) Romans 3:4 states, "Let God be true, but every man a liar."

In all my defense of the older generation in this book and in my first book, I must add that even though there are those who have attended church for years, many of them are complacent in a belief that they've "heard it all" and know the Bible. Only after a person has memorized the Bible from cover to cover, can he rest in knowing he's off to a good start. Hosea warned that God's people were "destroyed for lack of knowledge: because thou hast rejected knowledge, I will also reject thee" (Hos. 4:6). My main focus is on deception aimed at the younger generation, but Satan seeks to devour whomever he can, no matter the age.

We must also beware of the humanistic shift telling a person to "find his own truth" or "find what you believe and live by those principles." One Hollywood comedian said he didn't know whose boundaries he had crossed, but they weren't his boundaries. We also hear, "For me" it was good or "for me" it was really bad. Opinions about restaurant food are one thing, but when referring to religion, it is not determined by what is good "for me."

In a book entitled, *Emerging Worship*, the author refers to a certain "gathering" where the "worship of God is worship that they themselves shape." He further states the congregation is "free to design their worship expression in a way they feel is best for who they are."[1] God never left worship to our own discretion. His attitude toward worship has never wavered. In Leviticus 10:3 He clearly states, "I will be sanctified in them that come nigh me." He doesn't come "nigh" us, we are to go toward Him. All our commonness is only a sign our worship is somewhere near the ground and far from His presence.

The current dialogue-approach to discussing Scripture asks, "What does that mean to you?" Each person then discusses his personal take on a verse. Inevitably, secular humanism adds its voice from the ones who have not spent time in prayer and the Word. The abundance of the heart is shared........ TV, work, movies, facebook, You Tube, problems, etc. veering the conversation away from the Bible.

Our perspective should be, "What does God mean by this scripture?" as we listen to a teacher who has searched it out. Subtle shifting occurs when we decide to follow society in letting everyone be the teacher so all will be considered equal. Teacher and students now join in "sharing" as opposed to the old model where a teacher stood in authority as students learned with their mouths closed.

As a result, giftings are overlooked and "whosoever is willing" is put in places of leadership. (See 1 Kgs. 13:33.) A "leader" now has become a "facilitator" who only guides people rather than leads, letting them find "their own truth." The facilitator has the assigned job of getting everyone to enter into "the conversation." If there is no authority over the conversation, ideologies become integrated and narrow truth gets squeezed out. This method quickly shifts the paradigm from fact to opinion resulting in clutter and confusion.

The deficit in biblical teaching over the last few decades has left a very malnourished aftermath. Children who have not received spiritual truth to counteract global messages from their digital world are paying a high price. Alistair Begg of Truth for Life Ministries in Cleveland, Ohio preached that "the authority, the sufficiency, and the exclusivity of Jesus goes to the wayside in our churches and we pass to this generation no faith at all."[2]

One group's reaction to emptiness in our churches is the new group called "nones" who want no affiliation with church at all. This group is "on the rise" as the decline in religious commitment grows according to Pew Research statistics.[3] So, as churches try not to offend with dogmatic facts, they end up offending anyway when those seeking answers find none.

Trapped by a Good Thing

What is the very thing that stops Christians from speaking truth and standing up for what is right? What is it that makes it hard to draw a line? It is the fear of hurting relationship with others. We have come to believe that the highest moral act is to maintain relationship no matter what. Pastors have put a premium on human relationship. One reason the church looks like the world is because the church has "religiously" maintained relations with the world. Today's church does not want to offend. We fear men more than we fear God (Matt. 10:28).

It seems noble to maintain relationship. Satan deceives best when he appears as an "angel of light" (2 Cor. 11:14). He lures man into trusting something that sounds right and loving. Not offending people sounds right because, for the most part, we should not offend people. Satan has trapped the church, not with blatant defiance, but with a focus turned primarily toward people and love of community. After completely persuading us that relationship at any cost is godly, Christians are now ready to lovingly embrace every religion no matter how much that religion shakes its fist at God.

Shifting From the Name "Christian"

An article in the Opinion section of a local newspaper told of author Anne Rice delivering a wake-up call to organized religion. She said she would "remain committed to Christ as always, but not to being 'Christian.'" She said "in the name of Christ" she refused "to be anti-gay, anti-feminist, and anti-secular humanism." The article ended with her asserting Christ didn't fail her, but Christianity did.[4] This mentality reflects the downward spiral in fortitude for Christianity's defense.

As mistakes committed by "Christians" are dramatized and even listed with atrocities committed by ungodly countries, we must recognize the difference between people's failures and actual failure of the Christian religion. Biblical Christianity remains right. Weak-kneed "Christians" bow to the spirit of Antichrist if they concede with, "You know, I'm a little embarrassed to be called a Christian, too."

A righteous man falling down before the wicked is as a troubled fountain, and a corrupt spring" (Prov. 25:26). Jesus said, "Whosoever therefore shall be ashamed of me and of my words in this adulterous and sinful generation; of him also shall the Son of man be ashamed (Mk. 8:38).

Even Worse

Website: Beware of Christians.com

Four young men raised as "Bible-believing Christians" decided to visit 10 European countries. They view America as a place where "truth" has been withheld from its citizens. They flee to Europe to find what other countries already know and only hope America will one day learn. Many parents may have already noticed how their children are not loyal American patriots. Disloyalty to the US because of failing morality is one thing, but to turn toward Europe, and her even further decadence, is another.

Insidious strategy has misled these young proselytes. Television propaganda swayed them against local and national patriotism. Many like them are now ashamed of their heritage. They are quick to ridicule the regional dialect and local rhetoric of their parents. Rebellion has always been reflected in rejection of parents and home. But now it even rejects godly national roots.

Dissent is specifically against regional stands for godliness and Christianity. "Small-minded" Southerners or Bible-belt affiliation is belittled and shunned by mass media. Conservative, rural affinity is insulted. When conservative Christians finally cave to the will of unpatriotic and disloyal propaganda, a generation will easily abdicate America's sovereignty to the will of a "national community." (See 2 Pet. 2:10; Jude 8.)

Christians and the church, as a whole, are not recognizing the deliberate attack on traditional, old-schoolers. This group is the diehards in America who usually think independently from the masses. It's these people who are resisting the agenda for globalization. It's these who are not afraid to take a stand and use a gun to defend their rights. It's these who are conservatives, and for the most part, Christian. They make up the last frontier for propaganda's assault to successfully change toward its way of thinking. Recently, television and movie producers have designed settings in rural areas to entice conservative viewers. Then indoctrination begins as ignorance, stupidity, hostile belligerence, and narrow-mindedness are linked with biblical values.

The four rebels mentioned above wrote on their website that they are giving up on religion. They are "churched out" and just want to "go somewhere else and figure it out." They say what "Mom, Dad, and Pastor have expected" from them is something they should try to "get away from." They promote a film which advocates a whole new spiritual formula for life and stresses a person's willingness to change their definition of the message of Jesus.

They are most likely trainees under teachers such as Brian McLaren. A chapter in his book, *a Generous Orthodoxy,* is entitled, "Would Jesus be a Christian?"[5] His rationale fears "Christian" is too narrow and Christians must be "generous" because that's what Jesus would do. His converts ask, "Since Jesus is so generous. How could people possibly go to hell?" Jesus mentions hell 16 times in His teachings and it is not an empty place.

True to his character, Satan leaps at opportunity. If a true Christian says, "Truth is limited to the Bible," Satan's puppet stirs doubt with, "Is God limited?" This trick preys upon unsuspecting sheep. Focus is shifted away from the subject (narrowness of truth) and put onto God's power (which is not limited). *There is a difference.* The verse about straining at gnats (narrow truth) and swallowing camels (broad lies) comes to life when considering this new view inside Christianity (Matt. 23:24).

Jesus said to His Father in John 17:3, "And this is life eternal, that they might know thee the only true God, and Jesus Christ, whom thou hast sent." Where is the youth pastor who seeks to know the real Jesus rather than a new Jesus who tolerates all views? Jesus clearly stated, "I am not of this world" (Jn. 8:23).

Admitting We Have an Enemy

Is it "generous" to allow enemies in heaven? Is Judas there? Along the same lines, should we invite Al Qaeda to stay at the White House? (See Jn. 17: 12; 19:11, Ps. 109:7, 8, Acts 1:20; 25). The church deviated when it shook hands with the sentiment that there are no enemies. We have heard preached with passion, "It's ALL about relationship" without the balance of separating ourselves from enemies. (I'm referring to an overriding attitude and mentality that refuses any type of confrontation. I am not condemning the need for relationship or the need for being part of a community.)

Disagreement is now more wrong than doctrinal error. Sure enough, confrontation can be antagonistic and negative, but *there is a difference* when it confronts that which defies biblical truth. Confrontation for the sake of argument is wrong. Confrontation for the sake of defending personal opinion is annoying. It is confrontation for righteousness' sake that is missing. Jude calls it contending for the faith. Contending, according to the dictionary, is "to struggle in rivalry."[6] Rivalry indicates opposition between two sides. If we do not recognize enemies to truth, we will not contend.

David Jeremiah wrote in his book, *I Never Thought I'd See the Day!*, "The more unsuspecting or unbelieving a person is concerning the reality of spiritual warfare, the more easily he or she becomes prey."[7] In order to attach more prey to his belt, Satan erases any belief about enemies. Scripture is not silent about the battle aspect of Christianity. It is a daily effort. "Therefore we ought to give the more earnest heed to the things which we have heard, lest at any time we should let them slip" (Heb. 2:1).

Satan's strategy is not to conquer Christianity with brute force, but to offer love and justice so Christianity will lay down her weapons (sword of truth) and concede. Then he will pat himself on the back for winning without a fight and mock that Christians were too weak to even try. (This is the same concept written in the Communist Manifesto which planned to attack Christian homes and family until America fell as "ripe fruit" into their hands. From my years of teaching history, I found many young Christians did not even view Socialism or Communism as bad.)

True Christianity teaches that we are to love our enemy. But the new definition argues that love goes so far as to agree. Loving our enemy includes disagreement and confrontation when there is intention of saving a person from their error. If we become "friends" and "agree" with everyone in the world (that is a nice thought), then we put away our defenses and allow every idea and opinion to influence us. Other opinions automatically affect us when we do not resist them because wrong/unclean naturally rubs off onto right/clean. If we put away the "cleansing agent" of truth then it will not be affective. God calls a person who is a friend of the world an adulterer (James 4:4). In the same verse, he says this person is His enemy. It's ironic that the very thing we try to avoid with our open arms (enemies) creates an even bigger one (God).

Physically, we should be friends with other people. We are to love our enemies. We are to treat everyone around us with compassion and care. We should be unselfish in all our actions. Spiritually, we love and pray for (God's) enemies, but we do not *agree* with any enemy who denies God and His Son. True love seeks salvation. When parents love their children, it sometimes includes reprimands and confrontation. If a parent never confronts and only "loves" his child without negative disagreement, the child likely ends up in jail and eventually in hell proving the parent didn't really love the child at all. (See Prov. 23:13-14.)

Christians need not seek out enemies, they readily manifest themselves. Many in the Middle East spew intentions of annihilating God's people. They are our enemy because they are God's enemy.

David said in Psalm 139:20-23, "For they speak against thee wickedly, and thine enemies take thy name in vain. Do not I hate them, O Lord, that hate thee? And am not I grieved with those that rise up against thee? I hate them with perfect hatred: I count them mine enemies."

~~~

As mentioned earlier, the paradigm shift occurs when songs, creeds, and phrases fit Christianity AND humanism. They are finely crafted statements which fit all creeds. A. W. Tozer who aptly nails whatever he is trying to explain wrote:

> Religious music has long ago fallen victim to this weak and twisted philosophy of godliness. Good hymnody has been betrayed and subverted by noisy, uncouth persons who have too long operated under the immunity afforded them by the timidity of the saints. The tragic result is that for one entire generation we have been rearing Christians who are in complete ignorance of the golden treasury of songs and hymns left us by the ages.[8]

Tozer noticed this decline decades ago. Sadly, the generation he observed to be lacking in scriptural content has raised another generation completely deficient in their knowledge of Scripture. Today's Christian seems totally unaware when humanist slants are used. We dismiss just one drip of black into the gallon of white deciding it doesn't make any difference. Satan's strategy is to slowly darken the mixture until we can't see any difference. The mixing into gray makes it too hard to differentiate the parts. The two become "one." We usually take the path of least resistance and accept the mixture rather than confront because it takes effort........ and endangers friendship...... and is viewed as negative. I find confrontation to be one of the hardest jobs of being a Christian.

So, if a Christian decides to be bold and oppose the "lie part" of a statement, he struggles with indecision because the "lie part" is physically the small, "insignificant" part. It's just a little black drip in the bucket of white paint. Plus, the whole bucket still looks mostly white and clean. Isn't it best that I show "love"? Satan smirks as he gradually gains ground .... little by little, drip by drip.

We fail to remember in our vulnerable state of compromise and reconciliation that our enemy speaks words that are smoother than butter and softer than oil, but war is in his heart and his words are drawn swords (Ps. 28:3; 55:21). Discernment is to see what is behind the smile and what results from small deviations. Spiritually, we must see Satan with honey dripping from his words, yet an appetite whetted for the souls of this generation.

Satan's apprentices have learned from their master that deception is accomplished through trickery. He *acts* friendly to cause us to trust him. "The kisses of an enemy are deceitful" (Prov. 27:6). This applies to Satan, yes, in the spiritual realm. But deception manifests in the physical realm as it lures people for spiritual purposes. We must view men who refuse God's Word (however friendly) as enemies to truth. In all our defending, we defend truth not ourselves.

~~~

Christians are smiling back, winking, and flirting rather than re-futing false statements. (See Hos. 13:2.) Blatant drops of black paint which reflect eastern religion, pantheism, and humanism soak our hand-held devices, televisions, movies screens, and many times our pulpits. An immediate rebuttal to the TV by turning it off, especially in sight of children, would speak volumes. We must clearly define our enemy and stop stalling as we decide what we think we can tolerate.

In 2 Chronicles 19, Jehu, the prophet, asked King Jehoshaphat a question after Jehoshaphat had allied himself with the enemy. Jehu asked, "Shouldest thou help the ungodly, and love them that hate the Lord?" Not waiting for the obvious answer, he concluded his rebuke with, "therefore is wrath upon thee from before the Lord." Tolerance of God's enemies is not a light matter. We must face the fact "loving" them that hate the Lord is not taking the moral high ground.

~~~

To compel Americans toward convergence with all doctrines and to break down any walls the older generation may be protecting, *Good Morning America* invited two American vets to discuss their experience in World War II. It was an interesting story how these men have since met up with their Japanese counterparts and have become great friends. As the story progressed, the definition of "war" was summed up to be "a disagreement between friends who just haven't had a chance to meet."[9] Is that true? What about Judas and Jesus? They had the chance to meet and Judas was still Jesus' enemy in the end. Is it just that we need to get to *know* our enemy first, then we can be friends? Society's answer is yes. Notice how gently we are getting to *know* Muslims as their friendly demeanor is strategically given place on prime time. Does friendship change Palestinians' hearts to destroy Israel? Surely we learned that pacifying oppressors never worked in the past.

Friendship does not change the heart of an enemy. It may postpone the inevitable. But the day comes when the enemy, not the friend, betrays the other. Regardless of the new slant on American history which does not defend our past motives (especially concerning colonization), we can be proud of America's history. We have not been the one to turn on other nations, instigating war, but instead have come to the aid of others when enemies have attacked them. In most cases, we have endeavored to protect countries attacked by evil dictators. We have not been the usurper, but the one to defend from usurpers. America has confronted enemies when (evidenced by their actions) they have refused friendship. The principle is the same for Christians. We can be proud to be Christian in spite of postmodern ridicule of past mistakes.

Christianity is indicted for being the catalyst (the bully) behind all wars when, in reality, Christianity has been the defender against evil provokers of war. True, there would have been no war if Christian countries had not stood against the motives of men like Hitler. He then would have been allowed to do whatever he wanted. If the WWII vets had first befriended the Japanese in the 1940's, we would not have had war, but would be living under a white flag with a red target, conquered by the kisses of friendship, and voting in the UN as yet another pagan nation. Too bad for Satan history didn't turn out his way because most Americans back then knew not to befriend those who wanted them dead.

It seems odd that I need defend the concept of war. Americans of the past knew certain violations on the part of tyrants required war in order to stop their evil purposes. In recent years, however, defenders are labeled antagonists. If they would just let the dictators have their way, there would be no battle. The worldly rationale, not backed by biblical Christianity, is very shallow and lacks depth of understanding about enemy intentions.

In 1 Kings 20, Ahab, king of Israel, made an alliance with the king of Syria when he should have killed him according to God's instruction. In verse 42, God tells him, "Thus saith the Lord, Because thou hast let go out of thy hand a man whom I appointed to utter destruction, therefore thy life shall go for his life, and thy people for his people." (Notice how Ahab called the king of Syria "brother" in verse 32.) America and the church, too, are paying a high price (in souls) for allying with enemies. It's the ungodly beliefs of other nations that make the alliances wrong. It's the spiritual effects resulting from physical union that makes the agreement fatal.

The whole overriding motive behind the peace movement in the world today is so there will be no resistance to the charismatic world leader when he's ready to make his move. Satan wants total acceptance and mass hysteria in favor of his "man of change." The mentality of the world must be dominantly tolerant as this man rearranges economies, governments, and all religions to conform to his authoritative agenda.

The Bible cautions us to "believe not every spirit, but try the spirits whether they are of God: because many false prophets are gone out into the world" (1 Jn. 4:1). *Many* spirits, according to God's Word are wrong, and only *one* Spirit is right. Our chance of encountering danger is high.

The Shift Toward Inclusiveness

As one generation sings, "Your love and grace are wide," they sing from a heart that knows Jesus' sacrifice made salvation available to the whole world, but is given only to those who accept it in truth. Another generation sings it from a heart that feels there is no need to preach the gospel because all people will ultimately end up in heaven since Jesus is so inclusive.

We sing, "He will gather all nations..... all will bow....... He's the King." Those singing from a heart founded in His Word trust that, yes, in the Millennium, Jesus will be king of the Earth and every knee of every nation will bow. They understand rebels will bow without choice. They will be compelled to bow. Their knees will buckle. But it will be too late for their salvation. Others sing from a young heart that has not been versed in Scripture and knows nothing of a Millennium, but believes man will create a perfect existence on Earth. They suppose all will bow in allegiance to a "king" resulting in salvation for everyone. They dream of a fascinating, irresistible king who will bring unity and peace. They have not heard in their churches that "by peace" the Antichrist shall "destroy many" (Dan. 8:25).

This generation is accustomed to society's instant response to popular promotions. It is not strange for them to picture themselves as part of a huge crowd of mass hysteria. Mobs camp outside malls and line up for blocks to buy the latest release. Not realizing life could go on without such devices, they actually feel they *cannot* live without them. Today's average person lacks resistance to public advocacy. Majority opinion is not even based on usefulness or worth. It has been proven that anything can be pushed and sold.

Mass hysteria doesn't raise any red flags to this generation. It's part of life for them. Christians can test if they are crowd followers by analyzing what activities draw the largest attention and the most media coverage, then look around to see if they are standing in that very crowd. It's easy to see how a mark in the hand will be so "cool" to this generation. Anything which makes purchasing quicker and easier will definitely appeal to those who have already witnessed an easy-pay society. The conditions are exactly right for an "international community" to speak with "one voice" urging "world citizens" to be first in line to bring about world peace.

Christians sing, the whole world is reaching out and yearning for "your" renown and praise is rising and eyes are turning to "you." It applies to the Millennium when nations will gather and worship God (Mic. 4). But based on the Bible and history, we must question if the masses will actually convert *before* His coming. Actually, eyes will turn to the Antichrist and yearn for his renown before Jesus comes to rule for a thousand years.

The "great end-times revival" we continually hear about appears, scripturally, to be in favor of an Antichrist. The Bible is clear that the majority of the world does not ever accept the true Christ. Jesus' time spent on Earth proves a steadily decreasing group of devoted followers. (See John 6.) The *whole* world will never believe in Jesus. Praise may be rising in that particular church service, but as history has shown, the world crucified Jesus rather than praised Him.

~~~

In the book, *The Emergent Manifesto*, written by several authors, one asks, "Is our religion the only one that understands the true meaning of life? Or does God place his truth in others too?" He also writes, "If the Christian God is not larger than Christianity, then Christianity is simply not to be trusted..... Christ being the only way is not a statement of exclusion but inclusion, an expression of what is universal.... there is no salvation outside of Christ, but there is salvation outside of Christianity."[10]

How does the author explain himself around that statement? His answer is Jesus Christ is not just in Christianity, but in all religions. He is promoting a false christ since Jesus is not outside of Christianity nor is He outside the Bible nor is He in other religions. When the author writes there is no salvation outside of Christ, we feel he is safe. But he is talking about a christ found with other names in other places. *There's a difference.* This particular book defines inclusivism as: "a view about the destiny of the unevangelized [that] holds that all people have an opportunity to be saved by responding in faith to God based on the revelation they have... inclusivism argues that all revelation is saving revelation."[11] The trick of this statement is in the definition of "all revelation" which is shown by further reading to include other religions.

J. Lee Grady, contributing editor for Charisma Magazine, commented in his article, "A Squishy Gospel," about a book written by author Rob Bell, entitled *Love Wins*. Grady wrote that Bell "suggests that not everyone will realize it was Jesus they were praying to. The inference is that Muslims, Hindus or Buddhists will show up in heaven since they were responding to a divine impulse they didn't understand."[12]

In order to catch Christians off-guard, error persuades us toward inclusivism by suggesting God "can't be put into a box" and since "He's huge," how can we limit Him? Automatically, we back down and allow the twist to overstep its boundary since we don't want to "limit" God. Even though God is limitless, His truth (by His own established law) is narrowly limited to the Holy Bible of Christianity. Many who peddle this doctrine claim they are not universalists who believe *all* go to heaven. (They do actually believe some go to hell..... those who are adamant in believing truth is found only in one source and who refuse to open their minds to other religions. This group is seen as an obstacle to progress and should not be tolerated.) Adherents to the new inclusivism are identical to those in church history who beheaded the faithful martyrs. There is no difference.

It's troubling that many who are seeking truth by purchasing books inside Christian bookstores are being tricked with new interpretations of the Bible. Those who write these books, publish these books, and approve these books for sale in the Christian market are rewriting the gospel. God will not wink at their malice. Deception is seeking to devour many and has successfully and strategically infiltrated the inner chambers of Christianity.

To prove the dangerous attack on Christianity is real, I could quote more of the previous mentioned books along with several others. But my intent is not to give error a voice. (These books, by the way, are not drops of black paint into a gallon of white, but are buckets of black paint with a label that reads "white.")

The very trait which makes a statement true (ex. the Earth is round) is the very trait which makes it separate from everything else (square, triangle, oval, etc.). Truth disagrees with everything else. Everything disagrees with it. Truth is exclusive or it isn't truth. It stands apart. It's different. The dictionary says truth is accurate, it agrees with fact, it is sincere and has integrity.[13] Is everything fact? Is everything accurate? Are all statements sincere and honest? Can we, like one prime time news anchor said, learn from everything no matter how ugly it is?

It is impossible to combine and reconcile differing belief systems unless a person is living under pretense. Sadly, pretense will be rudely awakened on Judgment Day and will be proven false as it's defender suffers eternity in hell.

We see how the church has shifted, but how have we as individuals veered from truth? Have we compromised by listening to lies from public media, not knowing the difference? At the very least, we should tell our kids when the media sprays falsehood into our living room. They cannot learn discernment without being taught first.

We have blindly followed church leaders assuming they have done the searching for us. We haven't questioned what truth really is. In our avoidance of legalism and strict Christianity, we legalistically think just attending and participating in church activities will number us with the sheep.

My prayer is that God's people will discern the zealous efforts now opposing Christianity and resolve to stand against its invasion for the sake of this generation.

Chapter 8

Embracing Other Religions

For this generation of young people, the entire world is focused on tolerance for all people, all cultures, all ideas, and ultimately all religions. We are inundated with messages of how Muslims are "just like us" as they eat pizza or love their children, but differences are ignored. Overlooked differences are devastating to our welfare. Similarities cannot be a good thing if differences kill you. We can consider world religions in their common quest to better mankind, but it's the differences when compared to Christianity that sends their followers to hell.

A Visa commercial suggested, "Forget all the things that make us different and remember all the things that make us the same." NBC Nightly News perpetuated the same principle by giving results from the "most exclusive study ever" as a "revelation" showing seven in ten Americans believe their religion is not the only way to heaven. The study concluded most Christians did not believe Jesus was the only way.[1] If we are to believe this study, it is a sad conclusion to know seven in ten Christians are shooting in the dark concerning their eternal destination.

Whether it's Oprah or ABC News recommending works by Desmond Tutu, Eckhart Tolle, or Deepak Chopra, or whether it's a "public announcement" by the emergent church, the message is one and the same. There is no difference as they press Christianity to welcome others by embracing divergence and to give up her "hostility" toward those who disagree.

~~~

A popular TV series ended its season, not only with spiritualism, but with explanations for its mysterious storyline. It culminated its saga with its view of the afterlife. As the characters gathered into a church, the camera remained on a stained glass window in the background showing six plates. One plate had a Christian cross, another a yin yang. There was a Jewish star, the Buddhist wheel, a Hindu "aum," and, finally, the star and crescent of Islam. The popular series then presented the message that people are not just leaving when they die, but moving on.

The characters in the "church of all religions" hugged and cried as soft, peaceful music resonated in the background. As one of the main characters (who had died on the final episode) was leaving through a doorway, he approached a bright light indicating he was entering heaven. The peaceful music, the feeling of unity, and the happy ending, in reality, was a story of how *Lost* the characters were as they hoped they were trusting the right thing.

Hopefully, Christians recognize this error and refuse to watch such contradictions to God's Word. But to think this falsity is praised in Christian literature would be pushing it. Right? How could this openness to other faiths come into our faithful churches? How could my preacher be compromising with other religions? Jesus warned His disciples that strong deception would be the sign before He returned (Matt. 24:1-5). How much more deceiving is error when it comes from a trusted source?

Inclusiveness

The move toward global unity is so strong that without vigilance, preachers will unwittingly pepper their sermons with the doctrine of inclusiveness suggesting truth can be found in other "sacred texts" like the Koran or the Hindu Vedas. If truth (not just true statements, but truth itself) is in any other book, we could conclude that salvation is available without the Bible.

A preacher may say the truth and mean the truth in his heart, but if he is too watered down or unspecific about what or to whom he is referring, young sheep of his flock will likely filter it through their world-view of inclusiveness. The narrowness of truth inside the Bible must be maintained in preaching because "gray truth" relentlessly tries to sidle into our midst opening the door for substitutes.

We can be assured the Bible excludes "others" from being sources of truth. John 17:17 tells us the Bible "is truth." The psalmist wrote, "Thy word is true from the beginning" (Ps. 119:160). The Bible of Christianity leaves no room for other fountainheads. All other texts are merely words of men because false gods cannot speak. (See Ps. 135-15-17; Ps. 140:11.)

If a man in the deep dark recesses of civilization has been saved without ever holding a Bible, his salvation came through the truth which agrees with the Bible of Christianity (Jn. 17:17). There is salvation in no other name but Jesus (Acts 4:12). We cannot attribute his salvation to "nature," another religion, or some other revelation. If a person ends up in heaven, he got there exclusively through the truth that is written in the Bible. He may have heard it rather than read it, but IT was the truth.

The trap for Christianity is in laying aside exclusivity in order to negotiate with other religions on *their* terms. Real truth can never bend in another direction because it's already in the right direction. Union forces truth to abdicate vital principles. Other religions have no intention of relinquishing their belief. "Their terms" is a reference to an article in a Christian magazine where the author argued, "if we are going to persuade a skeptical world of the gospel of Jesus Christ and make a compelling case for Christianity in this century, we will have to do so on their terms."[2] The author continues with accusations against the phrase, "the Bible says so." He feels this factual statement will no longer cut it. He proposes that Christianity has only been destructive with its "Us vs. Them" attitude.[3]

He is very persuasive concerning the cross of Jesus saying, "vengeance was canceled in favor of love" and "retaliation was overruled in favor of reconciliation."[4] He explains how Jesus' platform is one of forgiveness. Without doubt, love and forgiveness are tenets of Christianity. We are required to love all people of all religions as we draw them to "our side" and away from the error that leads them to hell. But he misapplies reconciliation at the cross to mean conformity between Christianity and other religions. He also leaves out the complete picture. God's vengeance was canceled for the Christian, yes, but not completely canceled for all as the nearing "Day of the Lord" will prove. We are already witnessing visible harbingers of that day.

In order to rid two-sided, confrontational language, one must put all religions on equal footing. I personally cannot do that since I know Christianity is superior and true. Other religions promise salvation, but do not deliver. I do not contend to win an argument, but defend the Christian faith because it benefits others to the saving of their souls.

The final blow in urging Christians to lay down their defense of Scripture is the compelling argument that "things are uncertain" in Christianity.[5] Satan knows Christians will not defend with confidence that which is uncertain. We must resist these attacks and rest in *certainty*. God's Word is "true from the beginning: and every one of thy righteous judgments endureth forever" (Ps. 119:160). It is very true that the cross brought love, reconciliation, and forgiveness. But for whom? Everyone? All religions? No matter what? Why did Jesus suffer if, in the end, all go to heaven?

Even though spiritual salvation is available to everyone, it is not an easy come, easy go, broad road. All religions may be similar in some areas, but when spiritual truths are compared, Christianity stands alone. Even if a religion agrees with Christianity in many areas, it is the area of disagreement that renders it invalid. Any Christian willing to accept other religions as permissible or even partially reliable is committing spiritual adultery and is violating God's first commandment.

Salvation from eternal death is available for all, but given exclusively to those who have faith in the truth of God's Word. True faith has substance and isn't just a nod in a general direction. Jesus/God died, rose again and is the *only way* to the Father. Other religions do not teach this. A person who does not believe the specific teachings written in the Bible will face eternal punishment. God will "take vengeance on them that know *not* God, and that obey *not* the gospel of our Lord Jesus Christ" (2 Thess. 1:8). The narrowness of Jesus is the "simplicity" of the gospel Paul talked about. He had valid fear that Christian's minds would be "corrupted" away from this simplicity just like "the serpent beguiled Eve through his subtlety" (2 Cor. 11:3).

Teaching Jesus' death reconciled all men (to each other and to God) without belief or faith is not the message of the Bible. We read in Revelation that judgment will result for any who reject His provision for reconciliation. A person must agree with the provision AND reject all others in order to benefit. If we abdicate what God really says for the sake of love and peace, it will be anything but loving and peaceful.

~~~

Error breezes by undetected because the church has been passive and complacent about *knowing* the certainty of truth. Avoiding clear, defined truth and opting for vague generalizations is a result of a famine of God's Word (Amos 8:11). Seeking to be accepted in today's culture, we have watered down the black and white aspects of the Bible. We shy away from adamant words like always, nobody, and never. Absolute language causes uneasiness because we've been trained to believe in loopholes of escape for every absolute.

We fear "arrogance" if we believe truth is specific and can be known. We cringe at being "religious" so we don't speak with certainty against the world's unrighteousness. We don't want association with holiness because it's "judgmental." Specifically designed accusations against our confidence causes us to gingerly lay down our arms.

We have welcomed more and more infidelity as we become less and less protective of truth. It's been said some Muslims have come to Christ by reading the Koran. Assured Christians who know there's only one view of truth are adjusting their thinking. Old "assumptions" are being re-evaluated. We are persuaded that collaboration "sweetens what we already believe" and "collective strength" comes from other viewpoints. Many people are now commenting, "We can do more together than we can do apart." But being part of a group doesn't automatically make someone right (remember Elijah against the 450 false prophets). Think how absurd and impossible it is to rely on the notion that many viewpoints are "stronger" than one viewpoint, especially when only one is right.

Along the same lines, I heard a secular song, "Common ties are stronger than the lines we draw." Drawing lines and defending narrow truth (as the martyrs) are ostracized as weak. More and more it's deserving of punishment because it supposedly stunts the growth common ties perpetuate. We don't understand how Nazis murdered so many people until we see how they were persuaded the Jews deserved it. Years of propaganda turn majority thinking against any group they choose to annihilate until it even becomes a "righteous cause."

Under the disguise of a theology "of hope," new views in Christianity promote evolution of ideas, merging two incompatible viewpoints into an improved third option. But "convergence" of pure water and poison does not create a better mixture no matter how you look at it. Think how contradictory, and even fatal, it would be to believe differing viewpoints of gravity. Giving up truth about gravity just for the sake of peace is really no peace at all if that concession ends in deadly impact. It is obvious that the only right and true way to approach life, either physically, and especially spiritually, is to approach life truthfully.

On a side note, we must remember Paul's advice to be all things to all men. (See 1 Cor. 9:22). Christians should be the first to relinquish their *personal* viewpoints if discussing irrelevant opinions. We are to turn our cheek without defense when we are personally rejected or mistreated. Our views in everyday life do not matter. We should please others and conform to their desires, putting ourselves last. But when truth is at stake, let the sword of truth be unsheathed without shame.

The Right Kind of Fear

Christians are now accused of "closing their minds in fear" if they resist "fluid change" in doctrine that requests they merge with other views. However, "fear" about ambiguous spiritual unity is really wisdom. Disregarding that fear is costly. Wouldn't it be cruel to tell someone not to fear jumping off the edge of a twenty-story building? Fear can save a person's life. Fear would keep him from jumping just as our fear should keep us from changing already accurate doctrine.

Some public schools across the country have decided to implement courses that teach the Arabic language. Newscasts covered the resistance of parents who "feared" this drastic change. The coverage was introduced with the patronizing and condescending phrase, "The unknown can be scary." It's not the unknown these parents feared, but the known repercussions of such a curriculum. The world has always ridiculed Christianity and will continue to call Christians fearful, arrogant, judgmental, ignorant, and whatever else. No matter how tempting, we cannot let down our defense of truth for the sake of those who are yet to be converted to the knowledge of it.

The Way of Truth Shall be Evil Spoken Of

2 Peter 2:2

Following is another quote intended to shift Christianity:

> One of the most interesting dynamics of the present time is the collapse of distinction between the sacred and the profane. Contemporary society allows for the "holy" to be found in the most unexpected places...... 'The new spiritual awakening makes use of thought-forms, ideas and practices, which are not at all alien to the majority of Westerners. They emerge from an essentially non-Christian religio-cultural milieu, a milieu that both resources and is resourced by popular culture.' The future of Christian faith lies in its ability to inhabit this gray world, not attempting to "sort it out" as much as to be available to help others navigate and negotiate the complexities that such a dynamic raises. To "go with the flow" might seem a trite way of describing theological engagement, but a commitment to fluidity and a willingness to swim in the cultural waters rather than insisting on one's own paddling pool is a necessary perspective.[6]

Red flag? This author urges Christianity to blur lines between it and other religions allowing the unholiness of neo-paganism to filter into the holiness of Christianity, suggesting we find the holiness of Jesus in unholy places. He asks Christianity to swim in other pools and "go with the flow" rather than resist change. The author is confusing Christians with his soft rhetoric, tempting them to surrender their protection of truth, belittling them with insults of narrow-mindedness for "insisting on one's own paddling pool."

The Bible constantly warns against outside influences and is clear from cover to cover that Christianity is not to be infiltrated by other religions. Ezekiel warned God's people of judgment because they "put no difference between the holy and profane, neither [had] they showed difference between the unclean and the clean." As a result, they were consumed with the fire of His wrath (22:26, 31). Those advocating mixture have no appreciation for purity. Paul's words to Titus are fitting: "Unto them that are defiled and unbelieving is nothing pure" (Titus 1:15).

A different author from the same book wrote, "Christianity's idea that other religions cannot be God's carriers of grace and truth casts a large shadow over our Christian experience."[7] Demeaning statements automatically cause us to shy away from our defense. The "idea" grace and truth are only contained inside Christianity is not an idea at all, but reality. The very crux of Christianity (grace and truth) is not a shadow, but the very light of the world! The real shadow on Christianity is the "new spiritual awakening" preached by wolves in sheep's clothing.

Whether humanity likes it or not, Christianity is the only carrier of truth. The "idea" Christianity has exclusive rights to truth is but a stumblingblock to unbelievers. The fact Jesus was exclusive truth is what cost Him His life. (See Jn. 8.) Truth originates with God and is found only in the Holy Bible of Christianity. It is quite "arrogant" to say otherwise. The authentic truth, the real Jesus, is revealed to us only through His Word. Jesus *is* that Word (Jn. 1:1; Rev. 1:2; 19:13). He is the only carrier of grace. We cannot separate Him from His Word.

Jesus tells us the scriptures testify of Him (Jn. 5:39). Although there can be true facts inside false texts and a liar can make a true statement (Satan can use Scripture), Acts 18:28 tells us it is the Bible that shows us Jesus Christ. Anything contradicting this and suggesting there are other "carriers of grace and truth" can only be advocating a false, Antichrist.

Willingly Ignorant

2 Peter 3:5

The world's focus is becoming more mystical and enthusiasm for the supernatural realm is rampant. Christians, too, are thirsting for a new and improved version of spirituality. The weakness of our flesh desires change. So, curiosity and fascination for the occult and the esoteric are perpetuated as we open our arms to the new spirituality without even questioning its distortion.

After observing man's weakness to grab onto the latest craze, Satan has been sure to promote new spirituality as the coolest app available. The package is designed to affect as many as possible, sweeping away resistance with the tide of popularity. Any who resist are dismissed as old-school and out of touch. On a global level, it is currently surging forward advocating strength in numbers.

Christian fence-sitters try to keep contact with God yet do not want to miss anything the world has to offer. Their heart is divided. The very thing that will pull them off the fence and into deception will be the beautifully-packaged, chocolate-covered promise delivered free of charge by a compromised church. The shiny red bow around the enticing package is irresistible love which embraces everything.

If a "Christian" falls for the consensus view that truth can be found in other sources, then he has given proof that he never did believe exclusive truth. The whole point of Christianity is to confess, believe, uphold, and adhere to exclusive, narrow truth written in one text. Exclusive eliminates others. So, to believe the truth PLUS 21 others means a person did not, in fact, believe the truth. (Approx.

22 major world religions.) He did not "believe to the saving of the soul" (Heb. 10:39).

One truth contradicts 21 others. Discernment is how we know the difference between them. A person betrays himself when he believes anything can be true. It's odd how a person can physically admit a school bus is yellow and definitely not red, blue, or green. But fatally fail to convert this principle into the spiritual realm and see truth cannot be all "colors."

Be Ye Separate

Continually, Israel would serve the Lord PLUS other gods at the same time. Samuel told Israel to "put away the strange gods... and prepare your hearts unto the Lord and serve Him only" (1 Sam. 7:3- 4). Those who professed to be God's people "feared the Lord, AND served their own gods, after the manner of the nations" (2 Kings 17:33; Zeph. 1:5). In Judges 17:3, a woman said, "I had wholly dedicated the silver unto the Lord from my hand for my son, to make a graven image and a molten image..." How could she justify dedicating money "wholly" to the Lord while violating His commandment against making images? Three verses later, it should not surprise us to read, "Every man did that which was right in his own eyes."

A nonchalant attitude about God's jealousy manifests when we judge what is acceptable in God's eyes. Flirtation with the world leads to adultery. We celebrate Christmas AND Halloween. We have Easter celebrations AND secular celebrations in the same sanctuary. We aren't cautious about putting a difference between the holy and profane (Ez. 22:26).

When you get right down to it, most Christians today are participating in 100% of the same activities as the world. If an activity is questionable (few of the younger generation consider anything "questionable" since most do not know right from wrong as determined by Scripture) then a godly label is applied for "purification." The Lord asks, "Shall I count them pure with the wicked balances, and with the bag of deceitful weights?" (Mic. 6:11).

~~~

False religion mingled with Christianity is the same as making a golden calf. Notice the Bible tells us it was worshiped at a "feast to the Lord" (Ex. 32:5). God's jealousy has not changed and a divided heart provokes Him to anger just as it did in the Israelites' day. Actually, having the light of the New Testament makes us more accountable and therefore provokes God all the more.

The Bible tells us to "come out from among them, and be separate" (2 Cor. 6:17). Who is them? It is false religions and their practices. We are not living separate, but have chosen to include anything for the sake of relationship, peace, lovingkindness, and tolerance. We do not draw clear lines and are now guilty of crediting any view as "true in its own way."

Jesus said something we rarely hear. He asked, "Suppose ye that I am come to give peace on earth? I tell you, Nay; but rather division." Concerning truth, He came to bring a "sword." His Word is that sword and it brings division (Matt. 10:34-35; Lk 12:51). More and more we see how biblical truth in the world is what divides. Since peace and love are definitely part of Christianity, we need to discern when to apply peaceful measures and when to apply the sword of division.

KEY: The problem of disunity is really when other religions do not conform to Christianity. If all religions would agree with God's way, there would be true peace. (See Jn. 14:27). Christianity cannot accept "their terms." The world must accept "God's terms." If Christianity refuses her duty to uphold truth captured inside the "narrow way" and decides rather to yield to other perspectives, only a false world peace will result.

If God set up the world so man could do whatever he pleased and be guiltless as long as it was labeled "good," then we needn't worry about anything. We can just turn on the soft music like the gropers from the TV series and hum our way into eternity. However, discernment tells us that neglecting truth and calling evil "good" leads to woeful regret (Isa. 5:20).

Real Fruit vs. Fake

Many upcoming "Christian" authors are bold in their intentions to converge all religions into one. One book reads, "Those who argue that other religious practices, such as Buddhist meditation and Hindu yoga, can be used by Christians often cite the passage in Matthew 7:15-20 that argues that a good tree is judged by its fruit. The implication is that practices that produce good Christian virtues (Gal. 5:22-26) are acceptable."[8]

We could then reason that a murderer who smiles at his victim is not really doing harm since he first practiced a friendly virtue. In reality, good fruit is only the product of a good root. I remember a bowl of ceramic apples on the dining room table when I was young. Half were green and half were red and they looked really shiny and good. But knowing they were not really fruit, I chose not to take a bite. My knowledge of their fakery saved my teeth. It's not what something looks like on the outside that counts. (This is not justification for absence of outward evidence in a Christian life because, obviously, an empty bowl does not signify real fruit either.)

Spiritually, we are responsible to make sure our hearts are rooted in truth and that our outer fruit is real and not a shiny porcelain-coated counterfeit used for display. If it's a work of the flesh, or produced by man's religion, it is bringing forth "fruit unto death" (Rom. 7:5). (We cannot take this too far and say all outward fruit is "religious." Christians should be bent over with fruit, but it's the unseen spiritual root that matters.)

Beguiling Unstable Souls

2 Peter 2:14

Pointing to the "good fruit" of other religions without mentioning differences of roots into the "true vine" or into a corrupt vine is very misleading (Jn. 15:1). Fruit from a corrupt vine withers (Jude 12). It is merely walking by sight and reverts back to the age-old belief that all "good" people go to heaven. This doctrine seeks to nullify what Jesus did at the cross. Contrary to the new perspective, people do not go to heaven based on the "goodness" of their false religion even if this goodness is deceptively called the "spirit of Jesus" or the "love of Jesus."

Jesus made it clear He is the vine and we, as branches, must be connected to Him in order to produce the right fruit. Jesus said, "Without me ye can do nothing" (Jn. 15:5). (This verse also proves man does not possess hidden divinity.) Jesus *is* the Word of God, so a person cannot have good fruit until rooted into the Bible. (See Jn. 1:1; Rev. 19:13.) Christianity is the only religion that reveals the true vine. (See Jn. 15; Rom. 11.)

New literature asks, "Is the Christian God the God of All Religions?" Though that question is a waste of time, the "Christian" publisher decided to give it opportunity to stir doubt. Weaker lambs are led into a valley of indecision when the published answer is, "When human beings, no matter when or where, reach out to something beyond space and time, they are, whether they know it or not, reaching out to *the* God .... There is only one true God, so anyone describing the ultimate principle of the universe, no matter what the quality of the description, is referring to the biblical God."[9]

Reaching out to "something" whether a person knows "it" or not is not the same as reaching out to God. Personal salvation requires an active "yes" to truth, not ignorant groping. "And this is life eternal, that they might *know* thee the only true God, and Jesus Christ..."

(Jn. 17:3). (See also Eph. 1:18; 3:18-19; 1 Jn. 4:6). To describe a principle "no matter what the quality" is validating all beliefs and shows ignorance of God's unequivocal purity. Blind belief is an oxymoron. "A fool hath no delight in understanding" (Prov. 18:2).

False literature seeks to pry open our minds to lovingly accept Buddhism, Hinduism, Shintoism, Baha'i, Scientology, Islam, Astrology, Kabbalah, and New Age cults as weighing equal to Christianity. "A false balance is abomination to the Lord" (Prov. 11:1). The Bible warns against unequal yokes, "What fellowship hath righteousness with unrighteousness?" (2 Cor. 6:14). The Christian God is not the god of all religions. *There is a difference!* We must be vigilant and stand against the doctrine of the broad way which leads to destruction (Matt. 7:13).

Remember these are "Christian" books published by mainline Christian publishers. As I read them, I find nearly every page of every book is clear in its fatal message advocating truth in all religions and corresponding validation of all viewpoints. The books consistently bash true Christianity for its adherence to exclusive truth. They appear harmless and loving while Christianity is made to sound hateful and cold. It's exactly what Satan would write if God let him write a book. This is not the belief of one or two stray authors seeking vengeance against their childhood pastor, but an army led by aberrant thinkers who are ravenous for the souls of this generation.

More Spoiled Fruit

A local newspaper criticized Franklin Graham for stating that his prayer was not a prayer to the same god as the Muslims and Hindus. Graham said:

> None of their 9,000 gods is going to lead me to salvation. We are fooling ourselves if we think we can have some big kumbaya service and all hold hands and it's all going to get better in this world.[10]

The writer of the article then asked, "If the whole world prays for a common good, will no good come of it?" She ended the article with the comment, "Transcending the notion that only some prayers are the right ones might get us closer to the enlightenment we purportedly seek."[11]

As she demeans Franklin Graham, she implores Christians to "transcend" above their narrow notions. She, along with more and more open-minded people, believe joining all faiths is "closer" to truth than recognizing truth alone. But combining all religions for the "common good of humanity" is fruitless, if on Judgment Day, those who are "enlightened" are plucked up and cast into the fire.

Humanism : The Original Lie

The promotion of the phrase "fully human" is implying humans have worth, goodness, and ultimately God at their core. On the contrary, it is our humanness which separates us from God. (This is one reason why God became human in order to redeem us. There was no way humans could fellowship with God without a mediator.) I saw a bumper sticker which said, "Be Human." I guess the driver was trying to be negative, since being human has been the catalyst for chaos since the beginning of history. This kind of "hate-talk" must be more "open-minded" to the "change" that comes through repentance.

As in the Garden of Eden, humanism subtly lures toward treason against God. It points to a "Christ consciousness" within. It flatters with the idea that humans "embody God." Notice: I am capitalizing "God" to emphasize what new Christianity promotes. The Hindu concept of embodiment of a god (little g) is called an avatar, a word all-too familiar in American society.

Embodying a god is different from being the "body" of Christ. Christians are the body, Jesus is the head. A body is only alive with a head. Eliminating our head (Jesus), results in a dead body. The head is separate from the body. We do not become God at conversion. New Christianity teaches that a person can be awakened to his hidden "Christ." The "collective consciousness" of all religions is said to be the ultimate redemption of the world. Claiming Christ as a "consciousness" or "awareness" rather than a person, aligns with the spirit of Antichrist and denies Christ is a specific man of flesh (1 Jn. 2:22; 1 Jn. 4:3; 2 Jn. 7). "Christ" is not a state of consciousness, an awareness, a conversation, a force, or some type of energy we tap into.

> And every spirit that confesseth not that Jesus Christ is come in the flesh is not of God: and this is that spirit of antichrist, whereof ye have heard that it should come; and even now already is it in the world (1 Jn. 4:3).

> For many deceivers are entered into the world, who confess not that Jesus Christ is come in the flesh. This is a deceiver and an antichrist (2 Jn.7).

The book of Hebrews tells us of the "living way" provided for us "through the veil" (through Jesus in the flesh) into the presence of God (Heb. 10:20). Jesus Himself is the "living" way. We enter God's presence "by the blood of Jesus," not His love (vs. 19). It is the sacrificed "body of Jesus" (not our own) that provides for our salvation (vs. 5, 10). "This man" is the only way to eternal life (vs. 12).

Only Jesus is Christ. Nobody else is Christ. Christ is not separate from Jesus. Christ-ness cannot be attained through good deeds. We humans have no part in becoming Christ. We partake in Him, allowing Him to work through us (Heb. 3:14). *There is a difference* in partaking of something, as in a meal, and actually becoming that meal. In communion, we partake of Jesus' body and blood yielding our bodies as vessels unto Him. We "consume" His Word to be more like Him. But we never become Him. We hear people "are what they eat." But who really believes a vegetarian actually becomes a tomato?

When Jesus is seen in a person's life, it is because that person's "true self" (humanness) has stepped to the back and allowed Jesus to work through him. Jesus Himself still remains separate from that person. The spirit of Antichrist advocates "Jesus," "goodness," and "Christ" as original human characteristics which must be allowed to "emerge." Satan continually degrades and blasphemes the name of Jesus in claiming anyone can be Christ.

Redemption does not come through collective human acts of justice toward human suffering. Redemption comes only by "means of death" of Jesus (Heb. 9:15). Here is another paradigm shift: The older generation (in general) understands fellowship with God comes by Jesus' blood and acts of justice are a reflection of Jesus in our lives. But the younger generation (in general) believes these acts are themselves fellowship with God because they are rooted in love (to them an equal substitute for Jesus). The difference being love replaced blood.

Paul told us we cannot save ourselves because the gospel of salvation "is not after man" (Gal. 1:11). Access to God comes only by the one who conquered sin with perfect obedience. Jesus was, is, and will always be the only one who ever fulfilled the law through perfect obedience. This may sound like basic Christianity 101, but it's these basics that are currently under siege.

~~~

Jeremiah was frustrated with God's people (us) as they trusted in falsehood and followed prophets who prophesied lies "in God's name." They were met with severe judgment (true acts of justice) (Jer. 13:17-4:14). God commanded *His people* to "take forth the precious from the vile" meaning they were to separate true religion from false in order to experience true salvation and deliverance (Jer. 15:19-21).

Israel used false names for God. They used the "names of Baalim" to refer to Him (Hos. 2:16-17). Christians today have also shifted toward this faulty paradigm by adding other names to those defined to the Bible. (See Christian literature replacing His name with "Presence," "Mind," "the Haunting," etc.) Sadly, many new Bible versions have written generic names and, surprisingly, the NKJV has eliminated altogether the name, "Jehovah." Who would be crafty enough to erase God's names from the Christian handbook? That has to be the peak of cleverness if you wanted to erase His identity from a generation in order to deceive them later with a substitute.

The relentless pull in the spiritual realm toward global unification of religious beliefs is convincing. It is beginning to have power of consensus. Majority opinion moves people. As differences are ignored, all religions seem to have the same basic creed and the same basic "God," no matter the name. Many are unable to find truth as their conscience is seared by a gray world or they refuse to see exclusivity. Children struggle with the concept of unchangeable facts. Absolutes seem impossible to them. They live in a world of loopholes, change, and alternatives.

For years, Christian America has given alternative choices, change, and interchangeability too much recognition. We have been persuaded to move from the *didactic* (fact) to the *dialectic* (reasoning, logical, dialogue, the conversation) where everyone is the teacher and nobody is the student. As a result, true learning has been discouraged. We have ignored the concept where good is on one side and evil on the other. We have validated a socialistic faith which shares a collective approach to truth and requires all forms of theory to agree or face rejection.

God divided man's language and differentiated humanity after they tried to unify at the Tower of Babel (Gen 11:6). He did not tolerate an "international community" collaborating through collective human strength. Clearly, God is against global efforts for unification, especially under the banner of human strength and goodness.

God is Not the God of All Religions

New Christianity constantly repeats, "God is Love." We hear about love more than ever before. What does it mean? Is it the same meaning Christians held for centuries? No, because new love accepts everything. It labels nonacceptance as "hate." Is it loving when a parent knows about her child's abuse and just accepts it and does nothing? To claim God is love (which accepts everything) is what Charles Spurgeon said is making God obligated to His creature, binding Him by a law that says He is bound to give everyone the same treatment. Robbing Him of sovereignty, many do not want to admit His just nature because it is too horrible to comprehend.

The God of the Bible says in Exodus 33 and again in Romans 9, "I will have mercy on whom I will have mercy, and I will have compassion on whom I will have compassion." God is at liberty, without obligation to man, to do as He pleases. Knowing He drowned Israel's foe in the Red Sea rather than accepting them, we are to submit to the truth that He alone does what is right. In the future, when Jesus avenges cruel tyranny, enemies will not experience a love which tolerates, but will encounter quick and justified justice.

Spurgeon also said, "I do not know this new god that has lately come up, who they say is all tenderness and has none of the stern attributes of righteousness and wrath."[12] We must recognize that certainly, God is a God of love. But it would not be loving if He allowed injustice without recompense. It's the belief man has no sin nature that has led to the error that there's no justice in judgment or in hell.

We cannot abdicate loyalty to the one, true religion by conforming to other religions. It is not always best to go along in order to get along. Adultery will face justice before a righteous Judge and no excuses will be allowed. The excuse God has changed during the 400-year period between the testaments from a wrathful God to a loving God will not hold water because God never changed. He's always been loving and He's always been just.

Isaiah plainly wrote that unification with the world is a "covenant with death" (Isa. 28:15). Following trends toward world peace is making "lies our refuge" (vs. 15). It is hiding "under falsehood" (vs. 15). To agree with the good intentions of others' view of truth is an "agreement with hell" (vs. 18). Christians now have a choice to refuse this collaboration.

However, when the world actually comes together under one banner, the leader will make decisions based on a new philosophy of right and wrong (since real right and wrong will be rejected). Ironically, this "democratic" leader who "emerges" will throw out all freedom of opinion. (Interesting note: The dictionary includes "to rise out of the sea" in the definition of *emerge*. See Rev. 13:1- The Antichrist rises out of the sea.)[13]

No true salvation for mankind is found in united humanistic religion. For "the bed is shorter than that a man can stretch himself on" and "the covering narrower than that he can wrap himself in" (Isa. 28: 20). False unity falls woefully short of the global peace it advocates and will ultimately send its screaming devotees into the pit of eternal destruction to live forever alone without unity, community, or peace.

Psalm 83

1 Keep not thou silence, O God: hold not thy peace, and be not still, O God.

2 For, lo, thine enemies make a tumult: and they that hate thee have lifted up the head.

3 They have taken crafty counsel against thy people...

5 For they have consulted together with one consent: they are confederate against thee:....

16 Fill their faces with shame; that they may seek thy name, O Lord.

18 That men may know that thou, whose name alone is JEHOVAH, art the most High over all the earth.

Psalm 96

4 For the LORD is great, and greatly to be praised: he is to be feared above all gods.

5 For all the gods of the nations are idols: but the LORD made the heavens.

6 Honor and majesty are before him: strength and beauty are in his sanctuary.

7 Give unto the LORD, O ye kindreds of the people, give unto the Lord glory and strength.

9 O worship the LORD in the beauty of holiness: fear before him, all the earth.

10 Say among the heathen that the LORD reigneth: the world also shall be established that it shall not be moved: he shall judge the people righteously.

11 Let the heavens rejoice, and let the earth be glad; let the sea roar, and the fulness thereof......

13 Before the LORD: for he cometh, for he cometh to judge the earth: he shall judge the world with righteousness, and the people with his truth.

Chapter 9

The Exclusiveness of Jesus

There is a difference between Muhammad and Jesus. There is a difference between Krishna and Jesus. There is a difference between Buddha and Jesus. There is a difference between an avatar, the incarnation of a false god and Jesus, the incarnation of the true God. God in the flesh (incarnation) is *only in one person.* Only Jesus is the true, veritable, actual, genuine, authentic, absolute, faithful God. Scripture points to JESUS and the FACT that He is to be exalted above ALL gods, above Earth, above people, and above nations. His name is above EVERY name (1 Chron. 16:25; 2 Chron. 2:5; Ps. 57: 5, 11; 95: 3; 96:4; 97:9; 99:2; 113:4; 135:5; Phil. 2:9-10).

Jesus warned, "Many shall come in my name, saying, I am Christ; and shall deceive many" (Matt. 24:5). The word "many" should prick our ears. To avoid being tricked, we must compare. First we acknowledge significant differences between false and real, then take the next logical step and admit that because of discrepancy, two CANNOT be the same. Others cannot be Jesus. He is not one among many. He is different and set apart. Other names do not apply to Him. Other men, kings, prophets, or gods do not meet His criteria. On account of *fundamental* inconsistencies, other religions cannot meld with Christianity.

People readily accept fakes and shams when they do not practice discrimination. But when fakes are weeded out, it allows the "chiefest among ten thousand" to stand alone (Song 5:10). In a world without distinction, contradictions go unnoticed. Of course we should not discriminate between physical attributes of people, but we should discriminate between spiritual beliefs. If we avoid all "discrimination," we stop seeing differences where they count. Discernment has been one of the main casualties of our cohesive culture.

When we hear America has been "prideful" for her godly heritage, we reach out to other nations to prove otherwise. We read it's an arrogant assumption that God would choose to bless Americans over other countries. But American pride has not been in better people, but in the fact our God is better than false gods of pagan countries. *There's a difference.* Blessed is the nation whose God is the Lord (Ps. 33:12). It would be ignorant to think America has not been blessed and arrogant to think America's blessings came without God's help. (However, American pride has recently shifted toward boasting in her "resilience" and ability to stand in human strength rather than bow to God's judgment.)

Since we have not held a firm line, an inroad has been excavated by the Enemy. Public education, and even Christian education, has given inflated attention to other cultures, depriving American children of the knowledge of their own godly heritage. The God of America's founding has not been distinguished from gods of other cultures. Pagan practices have not been condemned or exposed. Ungodly customs and habits have not been shown to be manifestations of idolatry and demonic influence. Starvation and genocide have not been revealed to be results of countries' refusal to recognize the truth of Christianity.

Only the true God is the answer for every man of every culture. God is no respecter of persons and accepts every man in every nation IF that person fears Him as the one, true God (Act. 10:34-35). The gospel of Christ "is the power of God unto salvation to every one that believeth; to the Jew first, and also to the Greek" (Rom. 1:16).

Wells Without Water

2 Peter 2:17

Since the true gospel of Christ is not found in other "gospels," other religious belief systems are wells without water. (Literally, this verse refers to people who preach false doctrines.)

A true grasp of the gospel of the New Testament requires knowledge of the Old Testament. Men of the Old Testament walked by faith and were saved by looking ahead to Christ. Today, our salvation is gained through faith as we look back to the cross of Christ. Jesus has been the saving factor throughout all ages. Faith in Jesus is the actual "substance" of man's hope throughout all ages (Heb. 11:1).

In order for a person's faith to be saving faith it must not be shallow, negligent, or misdirected. Faith involves trusting Jesus as our only hope and believing His gospel stands alone. Faith is *loyalty* and *commitment* to the gospel's exclusive truth. *Faith* is understanding Jesus is to be distinguished from all others. *Allegiance* must be shown as we have no other gods before Him. True faith involves absolute trust and total acceptance of the true gospel's irreconcilable differences with other gospels. "Examine yourselves, whether ye be in the faith" (2 Cor. 13:5).

Idolatry

Anyone who does not acknowledge the true God is "without excuse" because His power is "clearly seen" and understood by the things which are made (Rom. 1:18-20). Nonetheless, man makes excuses and opts for alternate choices. Since the beginning, man changes the glory of God into the image of man (and even beasts) resulting in the worship of created things (Rom. 1:23).

Throughout history, man worships creation instead of God. (See Rom. 1:25). But there are differences between *evidence* of God's power as seen in creation and *revelation* of God through His Word/ Jesus. Created things are evidence of God. But Jesus is the very revelation of God.

Humans have "changed the truth of God into a lie" (Rom. 1:25). Created things will never be God. Creation is subject to God. The mountains tremble and bow before Him (Hab. 3:6). The sun and moon stand still before Him (Josh. 10:12-13; Hab. 3:11). "For by Him were all things created, that are in heaven, and that are in earth, visible and invisible, whether they be thrones, or dominions, or principalities, or powers: all things were created by Him, and for Him" (Col 1:16).

Nature is not God. "Seeing God's face in every sunrise" or "in the face of a child" is a popular theme today, but nature is only the messenger declaring God's glory and righteousness to man (Ps. 19:1; 97:6). A rainbow points to God, but it is not God Himself. A great architect's building may reflect ability and knowledge, but the building is not the architect himself. There is a big *difference* between the Creator and His handiwork which only declares His glory. (See Rom. 1:20; Ps. 19:1). A messenger is not the same as the one who sent him.

Even when Jesus was standing in clear view, men still didn't grasp they were looking at God Himself. Jesus asked, "How sayest thou then, Show us the Father?" (Jn. 14:9). God's love doesn't fall short if someone goes to hell. A person's unwillingness to accept the exclusive name of Jesus sends him there. "He that believeth on him is not condemned: but he that believeth not is condemned already, because he hath not believed in the name of the only begotten Son of God" (Jn. 3:18).

Throughout the ages, man has been guilty of choosing anything but the true God. Man is satisfied with wrong answers. He strives to do things his own way, on his own terms. He wants to be God. He misinterprets nature and worships it instead. He wants to hear smooth things, not right things. Idolatry has many forms, but it always includes putting something before God. It is a work of the flesh (Gal. 5:19-20). It's walking by sight rather than by faith. If man stubbornly refuses to acknowledge God, even his stubbornness is idolatry (I Sam. 15:23).

Since the Garden of Eden, there has always been enticement away from God. The first humans faced what was "pleasant to the eyes" and what offered "to make one wise" (Gen. 3:6). Now enticement is even more high-powered as we live in perilous times where delusion is strong (2 Thess. 2:10-11; 2 Tim. 3:1). Adam and Eve were charmed by an "apple" without much peer pressure. Today, we are enticed by lights and activity and what is "pleasant to the eyes" all the way from Hollywood to New York City (fittingly called The Big Apple). We are allured with a reward of popularity as we cave to peer pressure. In today's culture, reputation, recognition, and influence promises to "make one wise."

For the sake of relationship, and not offending others, we participate in questionable activities. But Christians should be the ones representing a stable moral factor in our culture, especially for children. Rather than relating to children on their level and acting childish, parents should bring children up to a higher level. "Quality time" in eternity will be measured with a spiritual stick.

If a person of a false religion sacrifices his life and calls it worship, it doesn't count because precedence is not given to the God of the Bible. It doesn't spring from the right root. It's as if someone who is not a city employee, cleaned the streets of their town then expected payment. But because they are not a city employee, their labor doesn't count for reward (heaven).

~~~

Our flesh (our way/our terms) must be offended before we can go to heaven. The Bible says we must deny ourselves and "sorrow unto repentance" (2 Cor. 7:9). Death to what we think is right is necessary in order to gain eternal life.

147

We think it's right for all to go to heaven and that "love wins" in the end. We (in our idolatrous mindset) think it is wrong that there is only one way to God. Yet, in spite of what we think, truth remains the same. God, in the form of man (only the man Jesus), suffered our penalty for sin on the cross, endured God's rejection and wrath in hell, and provided the *only* answer to man's desire for eternal life. His death and resurrection is the un-seconded provision for eternal life.

His atoning death provided salvation for all *who accept it exclusively*. It cannot be accepted along with other beliefs. It must be first and only. It cannot be void of acknowledgment and confession. Our mind and our mouth must participate in belief. A person must *know* that Jesus is the only way to escape eternal suffering. We must understand His death was a substitution for what we deserve for violating God's holiness. Man cannot change God's laws nor His provision any more than he can change gravity or the sun coming up in the morning. To conclude that it is "love," rather than Jesus' death which provided atonement, shifts our focus away from the cost and expense of His suffering. Focus is then placed onto an idol..... "love" which is separate from Jesus Himself. It shifts our attention away from the efficacy of His life-giving blood. It sounds so sweet, but it is so wrong.

With man's first sin, our corruptible unholiness and God's incorruptible holiness were completely separated. We lost access to God........ until God provided the way. Jesus *Himself* is that way. Today, entitlement and government socialism in our society has led many to think man is born into salvation and that all will be rewarded "no matter what" in the end. But man must agree with God's terms, not his own, in order to receive salvation.

To be an heir of the last will and New Testament, made effective through Christ's death (only), a person must acknowledge the singular provision (Heb. 9:16-17). Jesus' sacrifice was not an all-compassing reprieve over mankind regardless of how each person thinks or feels or knows or believes or worships or obeys his conscience. A person must believe to the saving of his soul (Heb. 10:38-39).

An example in the natural realm is the concept of a bridge. To get from one cliff to another, a person must step foot onto the bridge, trust it, and walk across. It should not be so hard to grasp the fact there is only one bridge. As we hike in the mountains, we walk on one side until we come to *the* bridge. We then cross over because of the availability of the one bridge. Jesus is like a bridge that crosses from man over to the Father. (In reality, though, He is not a bridge, but a ladder since man is not on the same level as God.)

A person who accepts God's terms must "die" (spiritually) to his own terms. By denying himself and taking up a cross, loyalty is proven. Each person's life is measured based on what he denies and what he accepts. If he accepts everything (without judgment), he shows lack of loyalty and is guilty of spiritual adultery.

Truth rejects man's answers. Truth does not go in all directions seeking common ground. Effort to create God's kingdom on Earth is human agenda. But the only way to come into God's kingdom is humbly, without an agenda. Trusting man's attempts to bring about His kingdom is the same as believing we do not need God. It is a Tower of Babel mentality. It is the same (as re-written history claims) as saying America's heritage was founded upon "cooperation" rather than dependence upon God.

How pitiful to assume you don't need a life vest in the ocean. How insensible to think you don't need water in the desert. How risky to go from one cliff to the other without a bridge. How blind to suppose man can create many ways to God, yet neglect the only way.

It Is Written

No Christian has it all figured out. There are many layers of truth in the Bible and there are "manifold" principles to be learned (Ps. 104:24; Rom. 11:33). This is no reason to throw our hands in the air and claim truth cannot be known. The gospel of truth is written in the Word of God. It is contained in a tangible place. It can be known.

It is not esoteric or hidden (although it is not surface, but found with time and effort). Truth is not a mystery even though mysteries are contained in it. Contrary to postmodern teachings which criticize certainty, even calling it idolatry, God *can* be known. To know Jesus (the Word) is to know God. Truth is "tangible" in the person of Jesus. We are, therefore, without excuse if we die ignorant.

Several months after the 9/11 attacks, former president Bill Clinton addressed the students at Georgetown University alluding some of the blame to America's "arrogant self-righteousness." He went on to say, "Nobody's got the truth..... we are incapable of ever having the whole truth."[1] Since the attack had obvious religious undertones, accusations of "arrogant self-righteousness" are intended to stop America's boldness in proclaiming Christianity. Christian nations do have the truth because they have Christianity. Disclaiming Clinton's assessment, we even have the "whole truth" because we have the Holy Bible.

In his book, *A Search for What is Real*, Brian D. McLaren wrote, "I am learning more and more to doubt with God, instead of against God."[2] Representing God as doubting anything is a direct arrow at His absolute omniscience. In McLaren's introduction, he explains:

> Instead of trying to tell you 'the answers' via dogmatic pronouncements, I would like to try to help you find the answers yourself. Instead of trying to tell you what to believe or focusing on why you should believe, my goal is to help you discover how to believe – how to search for and find a faith that is real, honest, good, enriching, transforming, and yours.[3]

Facilitating people to come to their own conclusions after offering questions about absolutes is nothing but seduction toward idolatry. People appreciate dogmatism if stranded in the desert without water. They do not appreciate a general, try-to figure-out-where-the-water-is approach. Also, I would appreciate specificity if I were about to step on a rattlesnake. Refusal to nail down truth's location hinders its distribution to a starving generation. It is beyond cruel. (See Ps. 94:4-6.) How strategic for Satan to lead people into wandering indecision until it is too late. Wandering without purpose in the form of wondering and doubt causes neglect of one's salvation.

Man is given only seventy to eighty years to make the one decision that will determine his eternal future. Satan seeks to cloud truth's location by first causing us to question it, then giving several options, then nicely suggesting we decide for ourselves what is true. McLaren ends his book, "I was actually finding my faith. Yes, I was in a sense losing the faith that my parents and church had tried to give me. But this was necessary, because I had to find a faith with my own name on it."[4]

Finding a faith with our "own name" is the height of arrogance. It's following our own rules. When a person dies then stands before God, He will only accept Jesus' name. Only that name will be valid. A person's own name will not receive authorization. The true bride of Christ will have one name, the same name. It is not a person's own name, nor is it the name of any other god.

One Means One

The true gospel is the Word of God and not the word of men (1 Thess. 2:13). Counterfeits may look real as they contain some truth, but they do not hold ultimate truth. As a door in a burning building may truly be a door, it may not be THE door of escape. Only the door leading away from the fire is the way of escape (Jn. 10:9). How inhumane to point to all the doors and say, "You choose."

Illogically, new theology actually preaches salvation is "in the name" of Jesus. But where it is DIFFERENT and quite erroneous (and very deceitful) is in the deviation that Jesus can have other names, even our own name. The Bible is clear, "Neither is there salvation in any other: for there is none other name under heaven given among men, whereby we must be saved" (Acts 4:12). "For there is one God, and one mediator between God and men, the *man* Christ Jesus" (1 Tim. 2:5). Other names do not fit the man, Jesus. Pluralizing the word "one" has devastating results and is impossible when considered soberly.

"One" cannot be sidestepped with clever, serpentine twists that demand Muhammad or Krishna or anyone else can be called "Jesus" or equal to Jesus, or even more deceiving, have the "same spirit" as Jesus. The spirit of Jesus is the Holy Spirit and He, too, only advocates Jesus as the true God. Jesus said the Holy Spirit "of truth" would "testify of me" (Jn. 15:26). Jesus cannot have the name Muhammad, nor can Muhammad be called Jesus. In the same way, God is not Allah and Allah is not God. *There is a difference.* We cannot combine their "spirit" since they are *not* the same spirit. If somebody comes to you from the east and another from the west, you cannot say they came to you from the same direction. (Unless, of course, you are deceived.)

The liberality of giving any god the name "God" is far from innocent as is giving any person equal standing with Jesus. (Christians are brothers and sisters of Christ, but never His equal.) God speaks of the day when He will end the pollution of His holy name:

> I will not let them pollute my holy name any more:
> and the heathen shall know that I am the Lord, the
> Holy One in Israel (Ezek.39:7).

There are two forms of blasphemy: (1) attributing some evil to God, or (2) denying Him some good which should be attributed to Him.[5] Giving Jesus another name or denying Him exclusivity is blasphemy. Adding unholiness to His holiness is corrupting perfection.

Seeing God in everything or seeing everything as God is superstition. It not only makes every petty thing "spiritual," but it presumptuously judges everything as of the right spirit, not even considering the wrong spirit. But everything is *not* God, nor does every cheap, common thing point to God. He stands alone, apart, separate, different, and above all things. There is none beside Him (Isa. 44:8). Spiritually, we must attain to His level, not think He stoops to ours.

Cleansing

True, God became a man. He stooped to our level, physically. But spiritually, Jesus' holiness and character did not condescend. He never sinned. He was pure. He was separate from others. He remained God. He came to make *us* clean. Paradoxically, He is a common man, yet He is uncommon because He is God. He's not just any man. He's THE man (1 Tim. 2:5). Because of its purity, Jesus' blood is the only cleansing agent capable of removing our stains.

Jesus' purpose for coming to Earth was to permit man's low estate to go higher. Atonement/reconciliation with God was the goal. Atonement brings man up to God. It was achieved by God being made lower, as a man. We have access to Him only through a mediator. Only God could do it. Man could never have changed his condition after he sinned in the garden. Our existence was in God's hands. His great love was manifest in the fact that He provided the way out of our helplessness. We must not distort the gospel by stopping short of Christ's atoning work and suggest He only came as a compassionate man who shows us how to live and love. Who are we to think we can ever learn how to live without a transformed heart?

To see God, we must look beyond the common. We must swim upstream and weed out the cares of life. We must seek the narrow way, not blindly follow what we feel is right. We must follow the Bible regardless of its ambiguity. We must agree with its disagreement with other philosophies. We, as Christians, cannot trust gut feelings about right and wrong because we do not "instinctively know" right from wrong. We are not born with intrinsic truth. Answers and truth are found *outside* ourselves.

Key: As error gains a foothold in our doctrine, remember the cleansing blood of Jesus REMOVES impurities, it doesn't make *everything* pure. *There is a difference.* Even though atonement purifies that which is impure, perfection comes by removing impurities. Jesus died to His own flesh. The "lusts" of the flesh must be slain and buried, not "justified." (This is a very tricky subject.)

Considering impurities: We could foolishly assume a chocolate cake recipe is very healthy because a teaspoon of spinach has been added. Instead, we realize the product is still junk food and, therefore, unhealthy. What if a cup of healthy spinach had only one-half teaspoon of arsenic? Would we ignore the bad and say it was still "good" for us? Concerning spiritual belief and where a person spends eternity, we must be even more vigilant against that which is bad. It's the bad parts (even in small amounts when compared to the good parts) that is killing this generation.

The world's dominant view is that man does not have a sin nature..... that our true nature is to love. Therefore, this generation feels no need for a Savior...... no need for cleansing. Even Christians have a hard time confronting certain behaviors because they don't want to admit they stem from rebellion. This is especially hard for parents who remember when their child was young and tender. The tendency of humanity naturally devolves, rather than evolves. We must first admit a problem. Then confront it, determining to solve it with the cleansing truth of Jesus. The purifying water of the Word (Jesus) is our only hope for redemption.

Atonement

Jesus provided atonement. He restored relationship between God and man. He is the mediator between God and man.

God is Spirit..... Jesus is Spirit/Jesus is flesh....... Man is flesh.

Jesus joined God and man. He made amends by diverting God's wrath from man and onto Himself.

However, there are essential points to this union. Nobody or no thing has atoning blood like Jesus. A person must partake of His "body and blood" in order to be clean. The result is *imputed* righteousness (Jn. 6:56; Rom. 4:22-24). Righteousness can be attributed to us, even though we are guilty, IF we partake in Jesus. It's not our own flesh or our own good works that make us righteous, it's His.

Only through the one, narrow way will it work........ acknowledging our problem then acknowledging Him as our substitute who received God's wrath for the guilt. How much more New Testament Christians should be obeying God's commandments and reflecting purity because Jesus' righteousness is working through us! If a Christian has no sign of righteousness, he has no sign of Jesus. A Christian cannot live like the world and claim he has Jesus because when a person has Jesus, he has righteousness.

God made the law that determines right and wrong. Man was under obligation to that law. Complete obedience to that law was man's only hope (before Jesus) and it was proven he could not obey it. Then Jesus fulfilled the law by obeying it fully. His righteousness PLUS His punishment for *our* sin seals our atonement with God. He covered all the bases. NO other religion even covers one base (of providing a pure candidate or appeasing God's wrath as our substitute). Only JESUS, the true mediator, can make men united with God. A person must confess, believe, and accept this truth in order to receive it. He can't just nod in the general direction.

Shadowed doctrine suggests what Jesus accomplished on the cross applies to all men regardless of their acknowledgment or comprehension. Advocating "don't worry, it's all good because God's love would never send anyone to hell" causes a person to neglect confronting his need for salvation. Just as a person purposefully chooses a route to arrive at any earthly destination, the way to God must willfully be chosen and "traveled." As Satan well knows, negligence and neutrality are costly so he only preaches love, love, love.

Let's say there are three boats: one going to Cuba, one to England, and one to Africa. A person on the boat to Cuba cannot be right to say he is on the boat to England. Only one boat sailed for England and he missed it. He is not going to England. How can new doctrine be so persuasive with such a shoddy tenet as "all boats are going to England"? Sadly, a person only realizes his error after it is too late and he has not arrived at the destination he intended.

In Christ Alone

In Christ alone, my hope is found,

He is my light, my strength, my song;

This cornerstone, this solid ground,

Firm through the fiercest drought and storm.[6]

Chapter 10

Impersonator

The concept of bringing two conflicting views into agreement is also called the "Third Way" or the "center." It is implemented for the purpose of mediation. It reconciles opposing parties. Both sides agree to concede. Without doubt, physical mediation is necessary between families, communities, businesses, and even countries. Physical mediation brings balance. Spiritual mediation, on the other hand, does not benefit from this concept unless the agreement is between Christians only. Christianity, reconciling with other belief systems, benefits no one.

Inclusivism advocates a Third Way as it promotes resolution between all views. It synthesizes irreconcilable beliefs into a third belief. (Politically, the Third Way joins right and left as they "cross the aisle.") It avoids essential concepts. It is a way that, on the surface, makes both ends of the spectrum "correct." It ultimately seeks to bridge truth with untruth forming one compatible system. Its persuasion is swiftly shifting Christianity toward a global center. It is most easily introduced into Christian churches who primarily focus on "relationship." Relationship (over-emphasized) embraces even error.

The two-faced doctrine is exposed when the difference between its "way" versus Jesus' "way" is understood. It's way is convincing because it is a peaceful "conversation" that only agrees and embraces. Its "way of Jesus" is a way that does not fight or defend itself (focusing on some of Jesus' actions in the gospels while leaving out others). Its random choice of Scripture does not completely define Jesus or His stand for truth and completely ignores the Jesus revealed in the book of Revelation.

Many contemporary Christian teachings and lyrics meet the criteria of the Third Way when they omit true definitions of love, the cross, the blood, redemption, salvation, justice, the way, and even the true meaning of rebellion. They provide neutral interpretations that fit gray meanings or even fit both ends of the spectrum. Some definitions are completely inverted, making good bad and bad good. (Many new Bible versions are a Third Way as they avoid critical language specifications.)

There is actually a *true* Third Way. It also works when *both sides give*. It is when God *gave* His Son and when man *gives* his life in surrender and obedience to God's will. They meet in the middle at Jesus. As mentioned earlier, bonds of agreement which blend all views are said to make a "stronger" way. But in the true Third Way, this bond only makes a Christian stronger. God is never made stronger after we join Him.

The false Third Way teaches people to *give up* their version of truth and "put themselves in the shoes of the person they disagree with most" and come toward another way of thinking. "Putting yourself in someone's shoes," *physically* for the sake of understanding, is not usually wrong, but *spiritually,* we need to be careful. Sometimes, the first step toward spiritual compromise may be a physical concession. Christianity, in shoes of compromise, is forced to abdicate its "exclusive truth" and embrace all other versions...... the very thing God condemns throughout Scripture. Christianity is the religion that suffers most when reconciliation between cultures is promoted.

Example: Christianity states a school bus is yellow, Hinduism says it is green, Islam says it is blue. The Third Way says we must meet in the middle and call it gray. It is Christianity that loses because it must abandon the right answer. For Hinduism to shift from green to gray does no harm since both are wrong. Satan, the driving force behind the false Third Way, understands the damage of compromise as he concentrates on forcing truth to concede.

Christianity cannot, in reality, meld with other beliefs. It is spiritual suicide. Reconciling two opposites (truth with lies) to the point of agreement is as ridiculous as calling a school bus gray. Saying it is all colors and they are the same color is an illusion. To assume salt and pepper are the same because they are both "granules of flavor" spits out a rebuttal when a teaspoon of pepper is added to a cake. To suppose up and down can "come together in agreement" meets hard reality when a pilot views them as equal. To say the left lane and the right lane can be "shared" hits solid truth after it's too late to stay within the lines of exclusivity. Reasoning that America should offer understanding and put themselves in North Korean shoes is the same as handing a hungry lion a piece of meat. Asserting that Iran and Israel must reconcile their differences is only a red carpet for the Antichrist to suppress Israel to his will.

~~~

The Antichrist will promote a Third Way. He will act as the mediator/middle way for global recovery. He will appear democratic, offering lasting peace and at-one-ment with all things. He will be a decoy who leads to spiritual death as he joins man with Satan's agenda. Rather than imputing righteousness to mankind, he will seal their doom with the mark of death. He will appear to fulfill the promise of unity and peace, but his doctrine will literally be the bridge to hell as puppets align in agreement to his methods.

What a difference between the true Third Way of reconciliation where Jesus joins man to God versus the false which joins man to Satan. There is a big difference between atonement with God through Jesus versus "at-one-ment" of non-Christians through the Antichrist to Satan. Satan is obsessed with violating the first commandment and urges man to seek at-one-ment with anything but truth.

As sure as Jesus knows who are His and not one can be plucked from his hand, Satan, too, will have in his grasp all who cooperate. They will fall as one screaming "community" into the lake of fire to spend day and night for ever. (The new false definition of "eternity" has been revised to mean: "just long enough to learn a lesson.")

Today, heightened interest in the mystical is shown as Judaism shifts toward Kabbalah, Christianity toward New Age, and Islam toward Sufi mysticism. The superstitious, secret, occult, metaphysical, immaterial, ethereal, and extrasensory fascinate this generation. Those unacquainted with truth will be easily allured with Satan's "magic" tricks. Like judges on prime time talent shows, people will be "blown away" as tears fill their eyes. We already see churches inviting these sensual performances. The Antichrist will be the most "qualified" messiah for anyone seeking only surface requirements. Jesus warned, it is a wicked and adulterous generation who seeks after signs and refuses to believe truth in faith (Matt. 16:4).

The world's thirst will be temporarily quenched when the Antichrist displays "all power and signs and lying wonders," imitating the miracles of Jesus (2 Thess. 2:9). Satan will even try to duplicate Jesus' resurrection. (See Rev. 13:3, 14.) The popular christ who *emerges* in the near future will be universally accepted and praised without question. Those who do question will be considered negative, out of date, and a non-progressive.

The real Messiah was, and is, despised and rejected (Isa. 53:3). David Jeremiah explains the Antichrist will rise to power as consensus pleads, "Give us a fine-looking candidate with a golden voice, a powerful presence, and the ability to enthrall people with vague rhetoric about an undefined better future, and we follow like sheep as the media bleats the candidate's praises."[1] He adds, "Completely overlooked is the substance of the man's program."[2]

Exclusivity, substance, specific truth, validity, and righteousness reveal the real Jesus. He is known through holy Scripture inspired by God. His identity is marked by crucifixion scars and a visage marred more than any man (Isa. 52:14). The blood and water which flowed from His side prove Him to be the true Son of God. When Jesus died, "one of the soldiers with a spear pierced his side, and forthwith came there out blood and water" (Jn. 19:34). 1 John 5:8 reveals the real Jesus is evidenced by "the spirit, and the water, and the blood" bearing witness in earth as they "agree in one"........ the one man Jesus. Not just any blood from any man qualifies. Jesus' wounds will be a convincing token to Israel as they mourn for Him knowing it is *that* man whom they pierced (Zech. 12:10; 13:6).

Jesus is the "bright and morning star" (Rev. 22:16). Lucifer is the "son of the morning" (Isa. 14:12). Some Bible commentaries write Lucifer as the 'morning star," erasing the difference. He will be riding a white horse. Who will be riding a white horse? Revelation 19:11 tells us the real Christ will be riding a white horse and Revelation 6:2 tells us the false christ will be riding a white horse. It's the difference between riders that determines the true savior of mankind.

We must recognize what Christ is and what He is not.

He is a Rock (1 Cor. 10:4).

He is a stone (Ps. 118:22; Matt. 21:42).

He is not a brick or any rock cut by hand (Dan. 2:34, 45).

The Rock is flint, not chalk (Deut. 32:13; Ps. 114:8).

He is pure, living water, not polluted water.

He is a Lamb and a Lion (Jn. 1:29; Rev. 5:5).

He is not just any vine. He is the true vine (Jn. 15:1).

He's not just another prophet or great teacher.

He is *the* Prophet and *the* Teacher (Deut. 18:15; Jn. 3:2).

He is not any star. He is the morning star (Num. 24:17; I Cor. 15:41; Rev. 22:16).

He's the unleavened Bread of Life, not a bowl of rice.

There are major differences between Jesus and all others. Jesus is the only one worthy to open the sealed book of judgment (Rev. 5:4-5). All proof for the real Christ is contained in Scripture and cannot be written here for the sake of space. Our job is to know *all* the law, the prophets, and the Psalms (Lk. 24:44). Our duty is to know what the New Testament apostles taught from firsthand knowledge. We can know, undeniably, the actual characteristics indicative of Jesus Christ so that we will not be persuaded by any other. (See Lk. 24:27; Jn. 5:39; Acts 18:28.)

~~~

False teachers in the church look just like any other Bible teacher. But they are different, not in looks, but in what matters – doctrine and motive. Wheat and tares look alike. Wolves in sheep's clothing appear to be sheep on the outside. Impersonators easily bypass detection when only partial knowledge is known. Con artists easily persuade anyone who is not concerned with inner motives and personal agenda. Roving theology goes right over the heads of those who are not doctrinally sound. In a world of tolerance and love, a flattering leader who exaggerates his results will be easily accepted (Dan. 11:21). People who follow him will not know specifics between truth and counter-truth. He will preach a mirror-gospel yet pass for the real Christ.

Truth has remained solely exclusive to one man since the foundation of the world (Rev. 13:8). Other "revelations" are shams built on assumption. We cannot trust a passive mentality that thinks God will automatically reveal truth to us (in different ways) depending on our "unique" situation or need. God does not change to fit us. We must seek Him, then change and accept Him *as He is* (Isa. 55:6).

To really know something takes time. Seeking takes effort. Distinguishing voices involves skill and practice. We cannot know God through casual acquaintance with Scripture. His voice is distinct, separate, specific, and narrow...... one voice. His voice is different from all others. We may hear many voices on a daily basis, but all are not true and from God. His voice should be the only voice Christianity will heed (Jn. 10:27).

Cultural Christianity has double-crossed this generation with its declining requirement of Scripture memorization and its abandonment of teaching on Sunday mornings. It has only contributed to young people's lack of discernment between the world's many voices and the one, true voice.

One day, I saw a red Ford pickup that looked just like my dad's pickup. It was the same year model and even had the same wheels (something I usually notice when differentiating vehicles). There was one major difference between this pickup and my Dad's – it was *not* my Dad's pickup. I could have climbed inside thinking I had the right to do so. I could then have been taken places I didn't want to go.

Little harm is done in not knowing the differences between pickups. But if this generation is taught, inside their churches, that they can apply "ownership" to other religions based on similarities to Christianity, they will pay a high price the day they realize it's not the true Father in the driver's seat. They will find themselves in places they never intended to go.

Satan is the master at maintaining an appearance of still being true. He has managed to persuade Christians they can *make* anything and everything "true" just by calling it truth or wanting it to be true. We see no harm in preachers saying whatever they please. We really don't give much thought when prophets "become wind" (Jer. 5:13). We trust Christian literature because it's supposed to be true. We put confidence in Christian teachers without skepticism just because they have a friendly demeanor and a good sense of humor.

Christian authors who sympathize with skewed theology can be rated by degrees. Some implement only parts of error while others jump at false teachings whole-heartedly. There are different levels of shifting. Some are not actual wolves, but are listening to wolves. Some are baby wolves learning the tricks of the trade. Others are, without doubt, leaders of the pack. Sadly, even leaders with good intentions, are being betrayed by these "home-grown" terrorists.

For the most part, we don't even question ourselves or our motives because we live in a culture that ignores infraction. We have adopted the world's "situation ethics" which denies judgment and justifies every motive. If pressure to do right is too high or uncomfortable, we cave. There is now unprecedented compromise with sin as Christians yield under cultural pressure and disregard violations against God's Word.

According to John MacArthur's book, *The Truth War*, "some might try to excuse such an outward act under pressure, as long as he didn't deny Christ in his heart."[3] Christians justify living like the world outwardly, while assuming obedience to Christ inwardly. We claim we would never deny the truth of Jesus. But...........

We choose relationship over truth. We give credibility to consensus views and neglect the credibility of unchanging truth in God's Word. We change definitions of what was always wrong and now call it OK. We agree with inclusiveness rather than being separate. We weep over children who are starving, physically, but don't even see those who are starving, spiritually. Unfortunately, lack of outward devotion only reveals inward denial.

~~~

The day has now arrived where strong delusion dominates world thinking (2 Thess. 2:11). Christians can no longer live with the mindset that truth is spreading, but that it must be defended and protected from seduction and extermination. The trump card of the false christ will be his agenda will appear truthful and his devotees will believe love is the only criteria. He'll quote scriptures like a seasoned pro. He will quote all the right people...... even pillars in the church. Yet, he will only be a mere imitation, a counterfeit, a fake. He will be the furthest thing from real. His aberration is what makes all the difference. He will, in fact, be the opposite of Christ....... Antichrist. He will be an agent of Satan of whom it is written, "There is no truth in him" (Jn. 8:44). He will be granted a "reign of terror" because his fan base has no discernment.

My concern is for non-Christians who will be swept away with end-times delusion, but especially for a generation raised in church who are sitting ducks for a religion that throws out the rule book. As seeker-sensitive churches have recently (deceptively) shifted back toward teachings centered on Jesus, an "appearance" of truth is emerging. But we hear, "You don't need to know the facts about the Bible, you just need to know Jesus." Or we hear, "All you need is a relationship with Jesus." True, *all* we need to know is Jesus. But the deviation is in thinking we can know Him without the Bible. A person cannot have true relationship without the rules.

We hear it's religion's rules that kills relationship with God. We must not conform to new morality and its 4-letter words such as "rule." Ironically, a relationship with Christ cannot come without religion (the right religion) and its specific rules for salvation. As politically incorrect as that is in today's church, we must obey the "rules" of salvation. A person cannot have Jesus by his own definition. A person cannot come to God on his own terms.

We hear it's religion that gets in our way, but it is that misconception that preaches we can have Jesus by any route. Scripture is clear we must come in at THE DOOR, not around it, not under it, or through any other. If a person practices contrary to Scripture, his religion is false. We can only say (in the church) "religion is wrong" if we are referring to man's religion. Biblical religion, on the other hand, is right religion. *There's a difference.* (Remember: The true definition of religion is a "system of beliefs" whether right or wrong.)

When Scripture is tossed aside and descriptions of Jesus fit only what we want Him to be (loving, tolerant, gentle, compassionate), then Christianity steps one step further from the saving knowledge of Jesus. We must contend for the Bible and for Christianity as the only *religion* that reveals the true Jesus. We cannot deny that Christianity is a religion or we will turn back in the day of battle because there will be no creed ("system of beliefs") to defend (See Ps. 78:9-10.)

The "knowledge of the glory of God [is] in the face of Jesus Christ" (2 Cor. 4:6). First, we realize there is a God. Then, we KNOW Him/ Jesus through His Word. We must not fall short in knowing only there is a God or that He loves us. Even the demons believe the basics (James 2:19).

Little by little, the stand for truth has weakened. We have the attitude that we will buck up and fight tomorrow when it gets worse. Or we somehow think since technology is advancing, truth also is spreading. We accepted the slippery notion that Christianity was "not a religion." Then shunning our affiliation with religion, we are now evading "Christianity." Now our weak defense has caused the Bible to be set aside while we just keep "Jesus." This final crossover in the paradigm shift is a "Jesus" without Christianity and, thus, an open flood gate for another gospel and another christ.

Who Are Today's Pharisees?

Wrong doctrines are similar in their error. Humanism says we are born with God deep inside under all our hurts. Nature worship tells us humans, trees, and raindrops are God. Pantheism teaches

God is anything and everything and can be acquired through any avenue. *The Shack* tells us God can be any person. The world tells us all beliefs contain truth and all philosophies have common ground which ultimately lead to heaven.

Jesus could have kept peace with the Pharisees if He spoke to them on "common ground" aspects of doctrine, but He chose not to be so loving and gentle. He pointed out disagreement and contradiction in their teachings. Those who preach salvation from their own perspective rather than God's are the Pharisees of today. They peep out from the crowd and critically view the Messiah of Scripture, rejecting His authority and exclusive teachings. They are insensitive to His holiness as they revel in fleshly alternative worship. They seek to destroy the only hope for mankind. They teach it is by human effort and global unity that we gain eternal life.

We have been taught (by church leaders) that a "Pharisee" is anyone who adheres to the rules of the Bible. But it wasn't God's rules the Pharisees promoted. It was their own rules..... their own terms..... their own definitions. (See Jn. 5:38-47.) Today's Pharisee twists Scripture and attacks Jesus by trying to "entangle him in his talk," changing written meanings (Matt. 22:15). New Christianity has "come together" with the world in criticizing obedience to God's rules and has glamorized a new perspective on truth. We cooperate when we overlook what Scripture really says.

~~~

Even though many other American (or English) women are named "Susan Seymour," they are obviously not me. Nobody would even argue another Susan was me because they can *see* we are not the same person. Nobody could persuade someone to believe two Susans were the same person. Even identical twins with the same DNA are not the same person. Even more so, the spiritual realm should be protected by Christians as we vow, Jesus is only who He says He is and cannot be another. As Paul proved Jesus was the "very Christ," we too should stand boldly in certainty concerning His identity. (See Acts 9:22; Jn. 7:26.)

If something doesn't look right in the physical realm, we are quick to notice. But we should be even more alert when spiritual unseen elements do not line up. Hebrews 1:3 tells us Jesus is "the express image" of God and in two other references, we see Christ *is* the image of God, not *in* the image like humans (2 Cor. 4:4; Col.1:15; Heb. 1:3). We should carefully protect even the minute details that apply to the very image of God. When Scripture speaks of the way to the Father as narrow, it means very, very narrow. It is Jesus, the one man, the one God, ONLY. The two-edged sword of Truth is VERY sharp.

Impostor

The illegitimate christ will be accepted without any recognition that he's an impostor. To his victims, he will be God himself walking the Earth. But this christ is without foundation or justifiable content. He will not be built on the rock. He will be built on shifting sand and circumstantial evidence. He will fit every creed, *but* the real one. Truth will exclude him. But truth is not the concern of his followers.

He will be an ever-changing chameleon who lacks the immutability of intrinsic value. He will have no inherent, essential worth. He will only be a cheap imitation. He will merely be a god without the "G" which makes all the difference.

Throwing out foundational teaching from the Old Testament and eliminating emphasis on the law, results in ignorance when viola-tion of holiness has occurred. The law first explains God's holiness, and second, exposes our inability to attain it, thus showing our need for a Savior. If forgiveness is given to me, without me realizing my violation, I flippantly disregard it. I simply live with a shallow belief that I'm accepted. Grace without knowledge of infraction and without understanding the high price to clear the infraction, is not appreciated for its true worth.

If a mindset doesn't understand the principle of holiness, there's no discrimination in what it will accept. If value is not the guide, cheap substitutes are welcomed. Holiness makes Jesus worthy of all praise. The lamb without spot or blemish is the only acceptable appeasement for God's wrath. Without evidence of Jesus from the New *and* Old Testaments, the false christ will be welcomed without reservation.

A first grader must learn ABC's before he can actually read. Basic, foundational building blocks lead to firm structures. In the same way, basic foundational spiritual learning is vital for knowledge of a holy God. A person cannot rightly build without the basics. If a person is given the end of the story (New Testament) without the beginning (Old Testament), he doesn't gain true understanding. If a person believes grace (New Testament) without knowledge of sin (Old Testament), he easily believes everyone is included.

The new world leader who only mimics a righteous cause, will be praised on the basis of open-mindedness and "relationship," not worthiness. He will conform to expectations by fulfilling a description learned in our church worship .... "beautiful, glorious one." (Interesting note: Antiochus Epiphanes, a type of the Antichrist, named himself "Ephiphanes" meaning "illustrious one.") Since this reference to "beautiful" is part of the picture, it does contain an element of truth. Jesus is beautiful when we consider Him, spiritually. But consistent with Old Testament teaching, He, physically, had "no beauty that we should desire him" (Isa. 53:2-3).

If not taught the whole truth about Jesus' characteristics, a person will not discern decoys from the authentic. Imitation Christianity with its many christs, its beautiful christ, its loving, embracing, and compassionate-toward-all-religions christ (yet fanged hypocrite) paints a distorted portrait of Jesus. It primarily focuses on His healing physical disease, but completely overlooks His preaching and teaching.

The new portrait is out of balance because it leaves out key elements. It portrays Jesus as meek and lowly, loving, gentle, and submissive to cruelty *only*. By this example only, Christians abstain from confronting dangerous beliefs, fearing they will appear unloving and "un-Christlike." *There is a difference* in Jesus' laying down His life for our sins and us laying down the right to preach the gospel of truth. Jesus Himself commanded we preach the gospel without apology, as He did. Many Christians back down from standing for truth when fingers are thrust (unlovingly) in their face, accusing them of not acting like Jesus.

Scripture is taken out of context as new thought manipulates the true cause of Christ and only points to one of His characteristics. One-sided theology stresses how He liberated women, helped the poor, and healed the sick. The fact that Jesus was nonviolent, never fought battles or killed anyone is true, but not the whole picture since His wrath, indignation, and annihilation of people, (including a woman called the "great harlot") is soon approaching. (See Revelation for Jesus' future action.)

As the screw tightens on Christianity's neck, Jesus' term for religious leaders as "snakes and hypocrites" is now flipped to refer to any Christian who resists inclusive doctrine or closes their mind to other beliefs. Rather, Jesus was referring to those leaders who avoided preaching the whole counsel of God, synthesizing other beliefs with Christianity. "Woe unto you, scribes" in today's bookstores who write literature that only proves "ye are the children of them which killed the prophets" (Matt. 23:29-31). It was these "religious leaders" who killed Jesus for His exclusivity. He was not referring to "religious leaders" who stand exclusively with Him and faced the same rejection. *There's a difference.*

The culmination of Scripture shows us although Jesus willingly laid down His life (otherwise it could not have been taken), He will return with fire in His eyes as He comes to judge and "make war" taking vengeance on them who have not chosen to follow Him exclusively (Rev. 1:14; 19:11; 2 Thess. 1:8). Fence-straddlers and those who take "middle" ground will be sorry. Human relationship will be insignificant and futile when Jesus' eyes fix on a traitor. Unlike His action on Earth the first time, the second time He will come to start a war and to finish it. *What a difference.*

~~~

Other religions' gods and idols are vain and baseless. They will perish in the time "of their visitation" when Jesus returns for true justice in the Earth (Jer. 10:15). Think of the differences between God and the false gods who cannot see, hear, nor walk. Can other gods form a man from dust? Can they make the sun stand still? Can they walk on water? Can they part the Red Sea? Do they have the keys to hell and death? How can Christianity merge with these weaklings?

Jesus' "name *alone* is excellent" (Ps. 148:13). He is the first and the last and beside Him there is *no* other (Isa. 44:6). 2:9). Jehovah is the "most High over *all* the earth" (Ps. 83:18). God's name is different and above every name (Phil. 2:9). It is not common. It is not to be used in vain. We should not use it flippantly, casually, or apply it to sentences without meaning. God's name is separate and cannot fit any person or religion. Other names CANNOT be applied to Him.

A Unified World

"How good and how pleasant it is for brethren to dwell together in unity!" (Ps. 133:1). The Bible speaks of the "common faith" and a "mutual faith" which is in Christ alone (Rom. 1:12; Titus 1:4). Jesus is the unifying factor, the real "connection" for a *true* brotherhood of man.

There will be a lasting global community when *the* Jesus of Christianity is the righteous leader of the world (during the Millennium). Interfaith movements (between Christians) seeking ecumenical unity (between Christians) can be reached as all Christian denominations of all nations are "one" with all who accept the specific, narrow way of Jesus. We can be diverse, physically, but united spiritually. This is the only true "unity in diversity."

All other religions have connection to each other on the very weak pedestal of assumption and rebellion. False religions may contradict each other in some ways, but at their root they are all seditious movements against God, unified by mutiny. All religions plus the Christian religion can never come together. To believe "unity in diversity" in this sense is not reality and any hope to "coexist" is a farce. Christianity's exclusive belief holding to the doctrine that "one" means one obstructs her relationship and cooperation with all others.

If all other religions would convert to Christianity, there would be global peace and unity. But the world is persistent Christianity must be the one to concede. We have been duped by tolerance propaganda to believe it is "fair" to include all schools of thought. The crack in the armor came when the new morality defined "including those with whom we disagree" as the highest moral achievement. But moving toward the center is not a noble act, if you are right and the shift only weakens your assertion and cheapens your stance. Inconsistent wavering between all schools of thought is the height of instability. "A double-minded man is unstable in all his ways" (James 1:8). Yes, there has to be balance in our Christianity. But there's a difference in tolerating what is within limits of Scripture versus accepting what goes beyond those limits. There is a difference in tolerating physical differences and accepting spiritual error.

Jesus is the Shepherd of "one fold." It is very *inclusive* to anyone.......... who listens exclusively to His voice (Jn. 10:16). Scripture states, "Also the sons of the stranger, that join themselves to the Lord" and choose His covenant, "even them" will God accept into the unity of His fold (Isa. 56:6-7; Lk. 17:18-19). I am eternally grateful for this verse because it includes strangers like me! Coming into the fold by "some other way, the same is a thief and a robber" who takes what is not his (Jn. 10:1). So, he cannot claim it lawfully. If a stranger refuses to agree to covenant terms, he will not be accepted into the fold of sheep (See Num. 3:10; 16:40; Lev. 22:10; Eph. 2:12.)

Spiritually, it's Jesus' exclusive name that includes us in God's family. It's the Jesus identified through Scripture, not any man with that name. If a person is betrothed to another, he will not have the right name. He may act or claim he is part of God's family, but when he is found without the right "wedding garment," he will be cast into "outer darkness" (Matt. 22:1-10).

Nobody can fake the "blood test" or the process of going through the mediator to get to God. Jesus Himself will be the judge and He will know who came through Him (Jn. 5:22). So we see, contrary to popular thought, it matters if you are "decked in white" on Judgment Day, wearing the right garment. (See Chapter 4, quote #2; Matt. 17:2; 28:3; Rev. 4:4.) Those wearing "strange apparel" will be punished (Zeph. 1:8).

Millennium

The "kingdom of God" currently depicted mimics the biblical millennium, but is false. Christians, for the most part, know Jesus will come and set up His kingdom on Earth for a thousand years. But they are shifting their facts because of what they are currently hearing as "the gospel." The plagiarism is very persuasive. The false "kingdom of God" will actually occur *before* Jesus' return and before the real kingdom of God. It will have seven years before it's facade is exposed by the true Messiah's millennial reign.

A kingdom which comes through collective human effort promises the same conditions as Jesus' kingdom. It assures "justice," "full knowledge of the Lord," the "desert blossoming," the "lion and lamb lying down together," and a "government of peace." This copycat endeavor is fueled by false love which tolerates new definitions for morality and rejects "rigid," biblical Christianity. (See Isa. 9:1-7; 11:6-10; 35:1-10.)

Recently, a resounding call for restoration of the environment through unified human effort has gained attention. But instead of this "solution," God will destroy the Earth with fire and judgment, then renew it Himself without human help. Can we not now recognize the early signs of God's final judgment of Earth as major earthquakes, tsunamis, droughts, and floods shatter records? The false god, Mother Nature, is licking her wounds as God puts her in her rightful place far below Him. (See Ps. 102:25-26; Isa. 13:13; Isa. 34:4; Isa. 35:1-8, Isa. 65:17; 2 Pet. 3:10, Rev. 6-16.) (Note: the land is defiled and judged because of humans, not from a sin nature of its own. See Lev.18:25, 28; Num. 35:34; Ezra 9:11; Jer. 2:7.)

World Peace

Society's romance with imagination has helped build a platform for false peace. Synthesizing all religions without distinction is fantasy at its peak. Peace without key components is not peace. The masquerade appears to work as we already see people putting confidence and trust in promises for world peace.

It is only after man's heart finds peace with God that he can find true peace and brotherhood with others (who also find God). Loving our enemies does not include brotherhood and alliance with them. Jesus said the peace He gives is "not as the world giveth" (Jn. 14:27). The world's peace is built on a faulty foundation that denies man's selfish nature. World peace is unattainable when jealousy, greed, and anger lie untreated below the surface. This peace does not recognize true enemies. (Notice the irony: As tolerance increases, shocking cases of bullying, road rage, rioting, and gang violence accelerate.) Jesus', on the other hand, accomplishes true peace because He gives a root cure for jealousy, greed, and anger.

Keep in mind Jesus gives peace as quoted above in John 14:27, but also consider Matthew 10:34 which states Jesus came not to send peace on Earth, but a sword of division. The sword of truth divides, separates, and discriminates. Ouch. As long as man has dominion over the Earth, Christians will lose peace with other views if they stick to the sword of truth. If a person loses his own agenda and carries a cross and does not follow the crowd of popularity, he will suffer rejection as Jesus experienced, firsthand, when popular consent nailed Him to the cross.

For the most part, we are to strive to live peaceably with all men (Rom. 12:18). It is not right to verbally combat people. A friend "must show himself friendly" (Prov. 18:24). With love and peaceful "conversation," we can attract people to Christianity. So, I am not advocating strife nor a life that does not seek peace. Rejection is not the goal. As long as Christianity is still tolerated, we must seek peace. But as our freedom quickly disintegrates and those who preach tolerance lose tolerance for Christians, we must be prepared to face certain rejection as we stand for the division of truth.

The Bible covers both sides of the coin. It brings balance. Instruction to love our neighbor *and* our enemies does not advise Christianity to go so far as to open our arms to other creeds. It does not invite us to turn our backs on Jesus. It does not advise us to "coexist" and smile at all choices. Signs of Christianity's concessions are manifesting in a generation who knows nothing of the dangers of covenanting with deadly enemies.

Social media and current news sources criticize a person who is obstinately and intolerantly devoted to his belief. He is labeled a prejudiced, narrow-minded bigot. (Remember, we Christians do not adhere to the truth of Christianity because it is "our belief", but because it is true.) John MacArthur boldly stated, "It is actually a sin *not* to fight when vital truths are under attack."[4] Vast approval is given for those who see all views as equal perspectives. Increased disapproval comes against Christians who stand for only one perspective of truth. Sadly, society's disapproval has only caused many to weaken their resolve.

God's love was exhibited to man through Jesus' sacrifice as Jesus set aside His glory for our sake. His provision for salvation is *available* to all men, all cultures, and all religions. (Inclusive applies to salvation in its availability.) Availability is then acquired through acceptance *and* belief in the exclusivity of Jesus as described in His Word, believing *all* that is written about Him from birth to resurrection until His eternal kingdom. It requires *rejection* of anything that disagrees and contradicts.

It is extremely shallow to advocate (inside Christianity) that God's salvation through Jesus encompasses all people regardless of what they believe to be true...... Or even if a person believes yet doesn't know what he believes....... Or if a person only believes God loves him...... Or even if a person believes in Jesus PLUS all others.... The new package has many labels.

To suppose a person really is worshiping Jesus as he worships nature or Buddha or any other "unknown" god, is to validate ignorance (Acts 17:23). Until GOD is declared, confessed, and believed, a person remains void of salvation. True understanding comes from a healthy fear of God (Prov. 1:7). A person cannot truly fear God until He knows Him. How do we know Him? We know Jesus. Fear of God evaporates when a person only believes God loves him (and the feeble definition of love is anything benefiting the flesh.) To think a person is actually worshiping God "no matter what" he's doing is promoting no belief, no dedication, and no acceptance of what is true. It is the gospel of unbelief and doubt.

The Bible asks, "For what if some did not believe? Shall their unbelief make the faith of God without effect? God forbid: yea, let God be true, but every man a liar" (Rom. 3:3-4). So, shall unbelief count the same as belief? No. Shall unbelief count and make faith not count? God forbid. Faith is the only thing with "effect." New doctrine, which claims to be inclusive, is actually exclusive when it excludes the one true faith. Its neophytes think they do not need faith in God to attain eternal life. They believe faith in whatever or whomever you choose will get you to heaven. God forbid.

Commandment number one: "Thou shalt have no other gods before me." We can only be safe if we believe in God without addition. To their surprise, new "ecumenical Christians" will be condemned by the first commandment alone.

~~~

God loves sinful man. He died for all men..... His enemies. He died for Muslims, Hindus, and Buddhists and is not willing that any should perish in their trust of false promises. Ezekiel tells us God has "no pleasure in the death of the wicked; but that the wicked turn from his way and live" (Ezek. 33:11).

To those (inside Christianity) who believe any opinion counts and all views are credible, combining all beliefs together into one, the Bible calls for division and asks, "How long halt (hesitate) ye between two opinions? if the Lord be God, follow him: but if Baal, then follow him" (1 Kgs. 18:21). The church cannot choose Jesus plus others. Everything cannot be true. We must choose one side or the other and if eternal life is what we seek, we must choose rightly.

Chapter 11

Indifference

> In those days there was no king in Israel: every
> man did that which was right in his own eyes (Jdgs.
> 21:25).

Having no king in Israel is not a good thing when you know, at that
time, Israel's king was God. When God is removed from a system,
every man does right according to his own standard. Without God,
humanism naturally fills the void.

Even though humanism dominates our culture and applies flexible
standards when expedient, Christians must adhere to an absolute
standard of right and wrong. We must maintain the rules that apply
to everyone for all time. Disapproval because we "stand our ground"
should not cause us to shrink back in weakness.

Tolerance

> For how can I endure to see the evil that shall come
> unto my people or how can I endure to see the de-
> struction of my kindred? (Esther 8:6).

As mentioned earlier, physical things are seen, spiritual things
are not seen. The evil overtaking Christianity is rarely discerned
because the invasion is spiritual. Even though physical symptoms

pointing to a spiritual problem are increasing, we tend to bury our heads and look the other way. A.W. Tozer noticed a similar problem with tolerance in his day. He said, "A new Decalogue has been adopted by the neo-Christians of our day, the first word of which reads, 'Thou shalt not disagree'; and a new set of Beatitudes too, which begins, 'Blessed are they that tolerate everything, for they shall not be made accountable for anything.'"[1]

Christians are, in fact, accountable for the downturn of American culture. We have approved that which is clearly wrong. We have not stood for truth nor resisted the dominant attitude of broad-mindedness which goes beyond its limits. We have apologized, conformed, and backed away from holding a line. We have adopted a light attitude toward God's Word so it won't offend anyone. We have not rebuked sorcery and witchcraft in our society. We have embraced all lifestyles and choices as legal. We have acknowledged everything to be "true in its own way."

As Christians, we must separate certain things, ideas, and activities as wrong, then acknowledge they will *always* be wrong. Even though every action is not listed in the Bible, the heart and motive is what counts and the spirit behind it must be discerned. We must resist certain things because of their absolute absence of goodness or value. We must "lay aside every weight, and the sin which doth so easily beset us" and not polish them off for use (Heb. 12:1). Even good things can get in our way.

In a tolerant society, a dogmatic stance is not tolerated, only criticized and mocked. So, leniency and concessions are destroying our youth to the point of no return. As Esther exclaimed, how can we endure to see the destruction of our kindred?

As Christianity changes her mooring, she is persuaded to consider what has always been wrong to now be acceptable. We question if proven facts (of the past) are now possible miscalculations. The doctrine of doubt blames the past for "erroneous" history, "flawed" classroom methods, and its most fatal accusation........ the "inaccurate assumptions" of the Christian religion.

~~~

Like a stop sign on a street corner, everyone should stop day or night, rich or poor, and even when in a hurry. In order to stay alive, those rules must be obeyed. There are not loopholes or ways to get around them. In the same way, man must line up with what God has established concerning right and wrong. Man will not get away with "running the stop sign" as he tries to rewrite the manual. The revised rulebook is deceptive because it asserts there is no stop sign (exclusive truth), and therefore, no consequence (hell).

The dictionary defines tolerance as the "readiness to allow others to believe or act as they judge best."[2] Tolerance works just fine if you are allowing others to fix a meal, mow the grass, or decorate their house. The list of where tolerance *should* be applied is very, very long. But tolerance should not be applied to heresy which results in eternal judgment. True love for mankind cannot allow that type of tolerance. (There is a difference when Christians "tolerate" other religions by not oppressing them and when Christians accept false doctrines as equal to Christianity. See Ex. 22:21; Deut. 10:19.)

The broad definition of tolerance embraces *everything* without the wisdom of stopping at the intersection. If we do not draw a line where to stop embracing, we will be blindsided by a forty-ton truck. We cannot show respect and credence to any god, nor can we permit right and wrong to be determined as one sees best.......... even when it claims to be for the "good of humanity."

In the following areas, Christianity can agree with her accusers that she is intolerant:

- ▶ The Bible does not allow people to think and believe as they judge best.

► The Bible does not allow other gods to have credibility.

► The Bible does not allow other religions the right to offer salvation.

So, Christianity and the Bible are intolerant where it matters........ for the good of humanity. Christianity is the light of the world and the way out of darkness. Only Jesus (of Christianity) is humanity's hope. The way to everlasting life is narrow, but possible, with God's provision.

To allow others to remain deceived because tolerance is put above truth is to allow them to die misguided. Tolerance, in this sense, is cruel and dangerous. Satan wants us to be indifferent toward error, sin, and wrong judgment. Satan wants parents to permit witchcraft into their homes. Satan wants Americans to condone blasphemy, profanity, and disrespect (he doubles his profit if it occurs in the sanctuary of our churches). He just patiently waits, holding in his laughter, until it culminates into another lost soul.

It's time for Christians to obey God's Word and "judge righteous judgment" (Jn. 7:24). We must resist detached permissiveness. We must not have the attitude "if it doesn't offend me, it must not offend God." We should be shameful of disinterest in the eternal destination of souls. If Christians persist in putting up with error based on the notion it is *right* to allow others to judge for themselves and *wrong* to impose our agenda on others, our mistake will be irredeemable and our attempts to hide our bloody hands futile.

It is "paradoxical" when the tolerance doctrine claims there are no wrong answers yet clearly defines what it thinks is wrong (exclusive Christianity). Exclusivity is currently associated with authoritarian rule and dictatorships. So, Christians who stick to their guns about where truth is found and believe others should believe as they do in order to go to heaven are as bad as dictators? No, discernment shows a difference. One is right (Christians) and one is wrong (dictators).

One cares about others (Christians) and the other about himself (dictator). We have definitely seen how a tolerant mindset has only caused our condition of decadence to worsen. What was once barely seen on a small scale is now boldly in our face. What was once shameful and hidden is now cocky and brazen. What was once in the closet now takes liberties and prides itself on its exposure.

Gradually, the things we barely accepted, then tolerated without offense, have now become everyday life. It's shocking to find how many Christians are participating in activities which were once considered wrong. Weak pastors try to reassure their congregation they are not against these behaviors so no one will think he is too stiff or uncompromising.

Liberal broad-mindedness is dangerous because it leads to involvement. Christians should take every thought captive because small aberrations grow into bigger ones (2 Cor. 10:5). Wisdom teaches us if we allow something on a small scale, we will ultimately participate. Understanding shows us if we ignore deviancy because "who are we to judge," the error will never be content to stay where it began.

Roget's thesaurus lists "tolerance" with the following words: broad-minded, liberal-minded, open-minded, inclusive, live and let live, condone, ecumenical, unbiased, wink at, overlook, shut one's eye to, ignore, dispassionate, indifferent, and detached, to name only a few from the list.[3] Do we want these characteristics when our children's souls are the price of our tolerance? Should we apologize for over-reaction? (which is usually not over-reaction at all, but mere disagreement). Should we continue to allow the media's mockery and scoffing at those who do not laugh at sin? If our spiritual eyes could see the desperate impasse this generation faces, we would not hang our heads in retreat.

Satan whispers with calm assurance, "Just let it go. What will it hurt? Didn't Jesus say, 'Love your enemies'"? But if we truly love our "enemy" (God's enemy), we must be kind with intentions of leading them to the *exclusive* knowledge of Jesus. If they resist and try to convert us, a bold defense of intolerance is in order.

Loving everything under the sun without discretion, including evil, is wrong because God *hates* evil (Prov. 6:16-19). Yes, we should tolerate all people even when they get on our nerves or when they disagree with our personal opinions (Eph. 4:2). But the aggressiveness of inclusive tolerance is not concerned with teaching us how to endure our neighbor's messes or our friend's high-pitched voice. The initiative is to set policy and ultimately bend Christians toward unification with other religions. Satan is relentless in his goal.

How many times have those who do not condone, celebrate, or congratulate something been accused of judging? People are even frowned upon when they just say something is not right. Anti-Christians expect Christians to tolerate and accept and defend "alternative lifestyles," "other convictions," "other philosophies," and those of "different persuasions." When we are pushed in this direction, a spiritual battle is inevitable. (Notice who really starts the conflict.)

If we have a Muslim or Hindu neighbor who "minds his own business," we aren't to go and confront, only show kindness with hopes of their eventual curiosity and conversion. But when he or she encounters us with false religion, we must state the truth in response. Nodding is easy, but allows the error to have the last word. If a gay person walks down the street, we don't have to oppose him, but if he or she boldly flaunts the rebellion to our face, we must defend righteousness. There is a difference in when we should and when we shouldn't confront.

If God's enemies adamantly refuse truth and only show intentions of keeping people from the gospel, then we can no longer continue to show acceptance. Kindness only enables them to continue in their error and influence others. In America's past, these encounters were rare since America did not resist Christianity. Today, confrontation is increasing as more and more wolves are pushing their way into the fold with intentions of eradicating Christianity's influence.

When teachers in the church teach a different "conversation," they are teaching the commandments of men and laying aside the commandments (rules) of God (Mk. 7:7-8). As good-sounding, loving doctrine implements all opinions, the devil prances in the next room. Nobody notices because the atmosphere is so kind. Open-ended, undefined teaching may sound right, and even biblical, but its lack of specificity is dangerous. Many spokesmen inside churches are adept in their ability to smile, flatter, quote scriptures, be humorously non-specific, and lead the spiritually-blind off a cliff. (They have great personalities.)

God is not tolerant: Jesus did not tolerate His Father's house being used as a den of thieves. God will not tolerate sinners in heaven. Jesus did not tolerate Pharisees and their pet doctrines. We, too, should not permit the new twist on Scripture which "widens the scope of salvation." Nor should we tolerate a "fluid" interpretation of the Bible which advocates change and "evolution of meaning" and refuses to state Scripture clearly.

Satan makes use of the fact we are easily "tossed to and fro.... with every wind of doctrine" (Eph. 4:14). We conform easily because it takes effort to resist. We readily go down hill rather than up. The human current naturally flows against God. Nonetheless, we *are* to resist by reproving the unfruitful works of darkness (Eph. 5:11). Our duty is to disagree with the indifference invading our churches. Becoming a "soldier of the cross" was never portrayed as an easy task.

Satan is always working to get people to the door of compromise. Instead of being coaxed into "just reading a book with a different viewpoint," we should remember God commands we keep His precepts diligently not turning to the right or the left, removing our foot from evil (Ps. 119:4; Prov. 4:27). When we refuse another viewpoint, Satan urges, "Just look at it, you don't have to agree" or he nags, "Just listen, you don't have to believe." This only works if a person is willing to voice disagreement after listening. But usually compromise results from leaning in the direction of error. Satan is not clueless about where small shifts lead.

As we read God's Word, lines become clearer between what we should tolerate and what we should not. True discernment involves knowing where to draw the line of intolerance. We tolerate until we come to the stop sign. Then we stop (with no intention of putting even a foot across) because proceeding further is detrimental as we collide with belief systems which run opposite to God's Word. (Other belief systems have no intentions of stopping.)

Compromising Truth

Is it Worth It?

Lines between right and wrong are gradually disintegrating as new perspectives dominate our culture. Since we have given assent to tolerance, open-mindedness, connection, and relationship at any cost, we no longer differentiate between a pure lifestyle and a worldly one. Far from being spiritually-minded and holy, today's faithful are remarkably just like the secular world. Culture has trampled over us causing us to buckle and accept its method of operation. We are found chatting about superficial subjects, avoiding topics on hell, judgment, and accountability. We are seen in all kinds of places, wearing and buying all the latest fads, praising the world's spotlighted, and laughing at anything that would cause our grandparents to blush. Yet, today's Christian claims closer relationship to God than any "rule-bound" Christian of the past ever had.

Spiritually speaking, illegitimate births are at the highest rate ever. Hosea spoke of *God's people* begetting "strange children" (Hosea 5:7). Christians (God's people) are guilty of spiritual adultery and, therefore, producing "strange" and unlawful offspring. Most children brought up *in* church are not taught facts about the true father. As a result, "many fathers" of untruth have staked claim to our children.

Error can have several faces (since it's not exclusive). One pastor allows Hollywood to influence his service, another sympathizes with New Age doctrine, others flirts with psychology, and then there are those shifting toward emergent sensationalism. Consequently, this generation (of churched kids) discerns no differences as they cooperate with whatever is presented to them.

We forget what Jesus said, "Ye are they which justify yourselves before men; but God knoweth your hearts: for that which is highly esteemed among men is abomination in the sight of God" (Luke 16:15). That which is highly esteemed does not provide answers even though it may seem the "way to reach kids."

~~~

A stand for righteousness, even in small matters, is lacking in the homes of Christians. Our unfaithfulness in small things reflects in our unfaithfulness in big things (Luke 16:10). God is not able to rely on contemporary Christianity. Possibly our weakness will bring Jesus' return (for judgment) rather than the popular belief our built-up faith will bring Him back.

God did not intend for us to come up with fun substitutes which keep the flesh happy and alive. He intended for us to deny ourselves and count the cost. Children must be taught the perspective that it would be better to be a doorkeeper in the house of God, than to dwell in the tents of wickedness (Ps. 84:10). Instead, we seem to have the same attitude as the Israelites when they said, "It had been better for us to serve the Egyptians, than that we should die in the wilderness" (Ex. 14:12). In the Bible, Egypt represents the world. We, too, desire to devour all Hollywood dishes out. We are servants to what social media offers and prefer it to the wilderness of not knowing what is going on in the world's viral gossip.

Jesus endured hardship and the cross for the "joy that was set before Him" (Heb. 12:2). We, too, can live heavenly-minded and not earthly-minded (Col. 3:2). We could avoid compromise if we would trust God and look to the end. We would change our habits and addictions if we were focused on eternal matters. We could change our culture if only we spent more time in God's Word than at the movie theater.

It's hard when we suddenly find ourselves in a situation we didn't expect would be compromising. Nevertheless, we must make the decision as soon as we are aware of the jeopardy, to get ourselves out by reversing "tolerance." It is not easy to walk out of a movie or to be labeled judgmental, but it is necessary if a Christian desires to please God and not bargain with the world.

We compromise when we say, "Oh, it won't hurt me. I can handle it." Today's Christian settles in his mind that he is immune to deception. The Bible advises us to be "wise unto that which is good, and simple concerning evil." Over and over the Bible tells the Christian to shun evil, to guard against it, to not even turn to the left or the right in participation, shunning even its appearance (1 Thess. 5:22). God knows the weakness of our flesh and gives these *rules* to safeguard against failure. Satan understands our flesh, too. He leads people away from truth little by little through compromise. His advantage is in knowing we find it easier to conform than to suffer rejection.

Gleaning the Good

We assume good outweighs bad as long as there is more good than bad. Or we sometimes change the application of bad like when we call something "wicked good." But natural cause and effect makes bad contaminate good. With all the mixture, today's Christian is unfamiliar with what holy and pure really mean.

We seem to find a good reason for compromise, especially when it's small. Compromise never comes without two consequences. The physical consequence affects you and others positively by maintaining peace, while the spiritual consequence relinquishes truth. A Christian has to decide if the "good reason" outweighs the truth he is forsaking. (I realize sometimes you cannot speak up because you are under authority, so the next option would be to silently walk out, forfeit attendance, or decline membership. Standing for truth does not necessarily require words, but it does require lack of agreement and participation.)

We cannot "glean the good" from yoga and only acquire physical benefits. "Any Hindu will tell you that there is no yoga that is purely physical."[4] We cannot say of a child who is reading Harry Potter, "Well, at least he's reading." We cannot justify movies as they promote Eastern beliefs, mysticism, and immorality. We can't agree with characters just because the lesbian or Hindu showed more kindness than the others. Unseen, spiritual damage outweighs any physical gain. It's like saying, "I don't care that I have skin cancer because I have a wonderful tan."

Lately, an *appearance* of correcting weak Christianity has been taking place. The social justice movement with its compassion, empathy, appeal for human dignity, and battle cry for equality seems to be a shift in the right direction. But it is still avoiding the spiritual answers humanity seeks. It is a mask covering the real issue. It is focused on kindness and cause rather than Christ Himself.

As the world possibly suffers more than ever physically, we cannot ignore the fact it is also suffering more than ever, spiritually. Christians must not be deceived in thinking we please God by merely meeting physical needs. As we help human suffering more than ever, we should see it as the avenue to bring spiritual truth into needy lives.

We tend to believe we can walk away from anything with only good results while bad just slips right off. It is blind to ignore weeds and see only flowers. If weeds are not eliminated, flowers will be choked out. (It is a shame we are quickly reaching the delusion where people are now saying, "Oh look at the beautiful weeds." The connection doctrine says they are the same as flowers. Even weeds are pure and good with this doctrine. This is where the verse applies: If the foundations be destroyed, what can the righteous do? Ps. 11:3.)

I'm not praising a nit-picky attitude or a negative view of life which ONLY sees the bad. *There is a difference.* The problem in the church today is in *never* referring to the "negative," avoiding a serious approach to the gospel, eliminating certain references in Scripture, and ignoring evil in an attempt to follow the world and its criticism of judgment. We must draw a line and admit there are some things with absolutely no worth. Some words, by definition, will never be godly terms. That which defies truth and God's Word has no value even when wrapped in a beautiful, shiny package.

While Christians are gleaning, they are decaying. While they dress snakes in pink tutus, sharp fangs are embedded in their legs. Satan delights in this predicament. Refusing to draw a line of difference only invites interaction. Opposites, right and wrong, harm and harmless are brought together as "twins." How else will the church accept the abomination of desolation in the holy place? How else will the world accept an opposite-Christ?

Forced ambiguity in our thinking pulls us away from a factual, "it is written," "thus saith the Lord," "the Bible says so" mentality. In other words, it shifts us from an unwavering stand for truth. We must not be afraid to draw the line and even be bold in our refusal to cross it. We cannot remain silent when a book, movie, or comment blasphemes God's holiness. We can speak up and say we will not read it or watch it even though the bad part is smaller than the good part. In today's culture, our righteous anger should be pricked more often than our need to overlook and tolerate.

When I taught history in a Christian school, one Christian parent was concerned when her son's class (in a public school) was scheduled to watch a video about Gandhi. She understood that this Hindu who hated the advancements of England's Christian influence would be made out to be a hero. She was concerned because she was training her son to see the error of Hinduism (bad part) and not focus primarily on Gandhi's devotion in leadership (good part).

Gandhi was far from being a hero since he advocated civil disobedience against Christian authority. In his devotion to Hinduism, he eliminated Christian influence in India resulting in a weakened nation and a fragile economy. He, physically, created misery and starvation for India's millions, and, spiritually, paved a road to hell for its citizens. We cannot excuse him with the tolerant statement, "He was dedicated to his people and only did what he *thought* was right." Similar movies and videos portray Nelson Mandela as a hero while they refuse to mention his Communist sympathies. Using the same approach, we could glorify men who flew airplanes into the World Trade Center and the Pentagon on September 11th. We could brag they gave their life for what they truly believed. We would be ignoring the fact that what they believed was wrong. Don't we want our children to identify what is wrong so they will not be enticed to do the same?

We readily avoid eating contaminated foods, but spiritually, we gulp down germs and bacteria. Christian parents are neglecting the principle of corruption as they allow their children to spend time with questionable activities or shady friends. Rather than encouraging children to "find themselves," we should point them toward finding God. If Christians would wear spiritual glasses for just one day, I'm convinced there would be weeping and wailing coming from many homes.

We lean in favor of the idea it matters what you focus on. The problem with focusing on good while ignoring evil actually allows evil to take root and grow (just like weeds). Ignoring an intruder in your home doesn't make him leave, he just takes more items or kills more people. Ignoring spiritual defects in our country only allows them room to push out righteousness and move our Christian nation further toward decadence.

After 6000 years of festering, humanistic belief dominates the world's thought patterns. It emphasizes good deeds just make bad ones insignificant. The world praises humanitarian aid and philanthropy and now the church is focused on human justice. But God counts even a speck of impurity as unworthy in His presence. Disobeying one of God's commandments makes us guilty of all (James 2:10). Man's guilt must be removed before good works can even begin.

There is enough of the cleansing agent (Jesus) for everyone, but that does not mean it is dispensed through any pump, well, or fountain. It is only found in one place. For example: We know laundry soap gets our clothes clean. We find it in one place in the grocery store. Sea salt and sugar may look like laundry soap, but they are on another aisle and they do not clean our clothes. Someone could exclaim they found potato flakes on the other end of the store and be excited that they also look like laundry soap. But only the real soap, found on one aisle, can clean our clothes. We can't simply believe it cleans our clothes. Only a conscious application of the soap to the dirt will get clean results.

~~~

Tolerance has caused us to view "mostly pure" as completely pure. We allow defects, spots, and blemishes as long as they are small. The purity gauge and amount tolerated is continually shifting its standard. Paul tells us, "Be not deceived: evil communications corrupt good manners" (1 Cor. 15:33). Corruption and infection spread when there is no battle against them. They defile that which is holy. The Bible is full of warnings against compromise for this very reason. A little germ does damage because of its capability of growing. Error has never been satisfied remaining small. It is like cancer which starts in one cell, then spreads throughout the body. It infects healthy tissue. It kills good cells. It is only stopped if it is removed.

God is of purer eyes than to behold evil. He cannot look at sin (Hab. 1:13). He sought a pure offering from the Israelites. But they did as they pleased, profaning the sacrifice, bringing that which was torn, lame, or sick. God would not accept it (Prov. 15:8; Mal. 1:11-13). They probably felt defects didn't matter as long as they brought something.......... anything. They may have even thought, like the tolerant mentality of today, sin and defects can be pure to God if we just "celebrate" them. But the very part which mattered was not the bringing of anything (sacrifice), but the bringing of something pure (obedience). (See 1 Sam. 15:22). Pureness is measured according to God's standard, not ours. "Woe unto them that call evil good" (Isa. 5:20).

We do not see compromise the way God sees it. We "snuff" at it. (Mal. 1:13). We don't see the damage it causes and choose rather to look at "benefits." Benefits of compromise are temporary, on the surface, and apply only to the flesh. The spirit does not benefit. It's a sobering principle of the Bible to realize God will give His own people their determined way, but will then send "leanness into their soul" (Ps. 106:15).

David prayed his heart would not be inclined to any evil thing or to practice wicked works. He also prayed he would not eat of evil man's "dainties" (Ps 141:4). He knew about enticement and realized the harm. Compromise usually comes in the form of a dainty dish. It's the whole principle behind shiny fishing lures. A trap waits beyond the enticement. David learned he could not glean the good or harmlessly accept attractive offers. A mouse is deceived to assume he can leave the trap with only the cheese.

~~~

The grass across the fence (from Christianity) promises freedom without boundaries and without "authoritative" rule. The lush grazing offers freedom from the narrow confines of obedience. Everyone in that field is coequal so submission to leadership is not required.

The greener pasture entices with safe-sounding "democracy" where the group pushes out sovereign rule. It lures with a "new rebellion" against established principles. It flatters with hope in man's "collective intelligence" rather than dependence on God.

The church is annoyed with confinement and traditional "rigidity." Christianity is even viewed as a "threat to democracy." Many church leaders want the fence removed between Christianity and greener pastures as they forget God's warnings about flirting with those on the outskirts. These leaders blight respect for the high office of pastor as they make it a common, silly, "crazy" profession that will try anything new. It seems they thrive to be accepted as worldly rather than godly. They do not lead away from dangerous pastures, but follow others into them.

Strategically, Satan has painted the dead grass on the other side to look real. The church looks, desires, then eats. Spiritually, we listen, then believe. When church leaders recognize man's "collective inability" and refuse to acknowledge the other side, they can then implement real answers as they listen exclusively to God.

The Danger

> And when ye spread forth your hands, I will hide mine eyes from you: yea, when ye make many prayers, I will not hear: your hands are full of blood. Wash you, make you clean; put away the evil of your doings before mine eyes; cease to do evil (Isa. 1:15-16).

We are quick to honor God with our lips, but our actions prove a heart far from seeking Him (Isa. 29:13; Mk. 7:6). Isaiah 29:13 points out our "fear" toward God is taught by the precept of men. Pastors teach us what to fear............ loss of relationship with the world. Today's Pharisee criticizes "churchianity" causing those inside churches to shun anything affiliated with Christianity. Postmodern fear of God is weak because it really fears man.

We are told, "people reject you, but God never will." We sing, "He will never let go." These are true statements for the saved. However, these songs compel anyone who is lost (a large portion inside our churches) to assume safety without conditions. Conditions? A person must first be ACCEPTED by God before he need not fear His rejection. After acceptance (God only accepts His Son's sacrifice), then a person can consider God's faithfulness. Before a person is accepted, however, he stands in the eternal state of rejection "no matter what" or how much he believes he is loved. What a difference.

Society and church psychology tell us our sin is only a reaction to hurt and mistreatment, not an internal cancer. Most preachers are silent concerning God's judgment or, even worse, misrepresent it in a light, humorous manner. As natural disasters occur at unprecedented rates and intensity, preachers should be pointing to God's pleading with mankind. God said, "My people know not the judgment of the Lord" (Jer. 8:7). Few hear God is a consuming fire (1 Pet. 4:17; Heb. 12:29). Fear of God alone could remedy the rampant adultery with other philosophies among Christians.

If only we could discern the impure teaching penetrating our church walls. Paul warned, we cannot drink the cup of the Lord, *and* the cup of devils lest we provoke the Lord to jealousy. God would rather us drink one or the other, not both. He rejects lukewarm mixture as He spews worldly church practice from His mouth (1 Cor. 10:21-22; Rev. 3:15).

Our conviction must be able to withstand Satan's tactics. He should not be able to persuade us to open our minds to other "truths." We must discern when he is trying to entice us with baby steps away from established certainty. We must see down the road where concession leads and not view compromise as insignificant. We must not be guilty as the foolish virgins who lacked the required vigilance and preparation (Matt. 25:1-13). We should heed Paul's warnings and not be ignorant of Satan's devices lest he get an "advantage" (2 Cor. 2:11). Resolve for doing the right thing comes through preparation and time spent in God's Word. It is *prior* to temptation that our choices *for* right and *against* wrong must be made.

We must stand strong as the martyrs of the past and refuse the neutrality of compromise. We must not "let go of certainty" to save our skins. They could have reasoned God's commandments didn't require suffering or burning flesh. But they were persuaded by truth beforehand, then staggered not through unbelief. They were strong in faith, giving glory to God only (Rom 4:20). They didn't hide from confrontation, but pointed out error and died because of it. They were fully persuaded that, what God had promised, He was able to perform and His Word was the *only* path to truth (vs. 21).

Instead of indifference, they believed that, in living or dying, they would trust God. Do we, like the martyrs, endure hardship for Christ's sake? Do we feel uncomfortable situations lend themselves to revision of rules? Do we preach "moderate" application of rules in order to squirm out from under legalism? After all, God created us to be happy, right? Or maybe it was God "created us for relationship."

Truth must be defended even at the expense of "sisterhood" or "brotherhood" (Matt. 10:35-37). Remember: I am not advocating a lifestyle of provocation or a Christian life without friends. I'm just trying to bring balance to our declining stand for truth. A person can truly be combative and provocative when they should have left well enough alone. Some people do look down their noses and "judge" others. I am not suggesting Christians stir up trouble. On the contrary, we should be peacemakers. But as a result of the world's propaganda, most Christians have become cowards. We should not be a know-it-all, but we should also be unafraid to speak up when something is contrary to Scripture. We can let some things slide, but others we cannot.

~~~

When we choose to ignore lines of separation and refuse to judge good and evil, we are not *really* avoiding confrontation or even uncomfortable moments. We are actually storing up future moments of discomfort. Satan continually tempts us, without mercy, with small concessions as forerunners to even bigger compromise. When a person comes to a crossroad decision, the tension eases when the easy route is chosen, but soon another fork requires even more compromise.......... all the while leading further from truth and into irreversible damage. It's easier to nip problems in the bud than to slay dragons down the road.

Sadly, in today's church, damage may not affect the one compromising, but will finalize in the next generation. (See Isa. 39:6-8.) The parent may be a true believer, but his complacency in raising his child proves costly. The world's dominant message is really getting through to this generation. But Christian parents are not really getting through to their children. Parents do not want to face the "bad" reality that since their child laughs at all the wrong things, does all the wrong things, justifies all the wrong things, admires all the wrong people, (and denies all the right things).......... he cannot possibly be a believer of truth and, therefore, an inheritor of heaven. Fools (unsaved) feed on foolishness. (See Prov. 15:14.) This generation will be shocked to find there are not blue ribbons for everyone on Judgment Day.

~~~

If we aren't sure something is error, then as responsible Christians, we must find out. We can't claim ignorance when Bibles are everywhere. One day, in God's holy presence, we will be compelled to honestly admit, "I didn't want to know the truth, so I avoided it."

To balance my message, we must put love and relationship *first* in our everyday dealings with people, *but* not compromise by putting relationship over truth when a moment of crisis arrives. We don't confront everyday. We may only confront once a year (unless we are a parent). Resolve is drawing the line, then refusing to cross. We should not be ignorant of Satan's tactics as he uses name-calling to bring about our retreat. He gains quick profit when we remove boundaries. He cleverly causes others' hurt feelings or a child feigning, "I didn't understand what you meant" to cause us to readjust our standards.

Attack is easy when there is no defense. The enemy has his way when there are no fences. But if there is a line, Satan determines to blur it into a gray middle of uncertainty. He is pitiless, creating doubt as to where lines should be drawn and how flexible they should be. But true defense always comes with strong lines and boundaries. Since our flesh so easily slides downhill, we must establish a strict regimen and stand for righteousness at every crossroad. Understanding where people get off-track, the prophets advised God's people to "keep judgment" between right and wrong rather than relinquish it (Isa. 56:1; Ezek. 20:19; Hos. 12:6).

When we leave an escape, caving is inevitable. Interestingly, once a person actually decides on a resolution, he finds himself backed into a corner with unyielding pressure. As soon as a Christian commits, opportunity arises to back down. This is what the Bible calls testing. If we stand the test, we are not legalistic, but faithful. (Real legalism, like new Christianity, adds pride, human goodness, and its own way to God's commandments.)

Many young Christians truly believe the Bible is only about love which embraces everything and judges nothing. Led by our youth, today's church is bending her ear toward the Third Way which joins all perspectives and finds common ground. It seems to be a wonderful solution to relieve friction and dissolve uncomfortable feelings. But it only changes God into man's image and believes He, too, compromises concerning truth. God forbid. (See Rom. 1:23.)

~~~

Jesus never compromised. He did not yield under extreme pressure to compromise when Satan tempted Him. At Gethsemane, He was obedient in the dark when no one was looking. On His last day, He did not have the support of one friend, even though they said they would not leave Him. When they denied Him, He stood anyway. Alone. His crowd of followers fell away. At that moment, He was not popular. Even then, He did not succumb to the uncomfortable circumstance for sake of relationship.

He didn't disarm. He didn't "make peace." He didn't choose friendship over mission. He didn't choose dialogue in order to learn other viewpoints. He, as *the* Word, directed His speech to bring "others" to the knowledge of truth and salvation.... toward His way of thinking. As man's only hope, He didn't fail. His sacrifice was spotless, pure, and uncompromised. He pleased the Father with every choice. He didn't make the slightest move toward placation or appeasement in order to stop His ultimate suffering.

He was tested to the limits and He was successful. He was not selective in His obedience. He did not look out for His own selfish gain. He did not choose to disobey if something interfered with His personal happiness. He submitted to the Father "no matter" the cost. He could have avoided crucifixion. He could have preserved friendship. But He forfeited the physical realm and was obedient unto death for the sake of the spiritual. (Paradoxically, He gained spiritual relationship with men, but lost it, physically, knowing which one was true and lasting.)

This obstinate, immovable Jesus is the type of man rejected by today's Christian mentality. Addressing this error, A.W. Tozer wrote:

> But something less is among us, nevertheless, and we do well to identify it so that we may repudiate it. That something is a poetic fiction, a product of the romantic imagination and maudlin religious fancy. It is a Jesus, gentle, dreamy, shy, sweet, almost effeminate, and marvelously adaptable to whatever society He may find Himself in. He is cooed over by women disappointed in love, patronized by pro tem celebrities

and recommended by psychiatrists as a model of a well-integrated personality. He is used as a means to almost any carnal end, but He is never acknowledged as Lord. These quasi Christians follow a quasi Christ. They want His help but not His interference. They will flatter Him but never obey Him.[5]

A false doctrine which compromises truth in order to gain the world does not profit if souls are lost (Mk. 8:36). Satan smiles and waits while indifference culminates into a deceived generation who perishes under his authoritative rule. His promise of democratic peace (yet authoritative dictatorship) will be one of the cruelest jokes ever played on mankind as he, like Hitler, outlaws all dissent.

Christians have not been equally aggressive as Satan and his willing affiliates. Perhaps we are not vigilant because we fear detecting a problem will require action. Maybe we have been molded to think there are no problems or seeing problems is negative and judgmental. History clearly shows Rome fell because they accommodated evil. It was a result of lowered moral standards, sexual excesses, and "a hundred cultures whose differences rubbed themselves out into indifference."[6]

We must not make the same mistake by shaking hands with enemies. We must separate ourselves "from the people of the lands," and not do "according to their abominations" (Ezra 9:1). We can't close our eyes, stick our heads in the sand, and claim we don't know how to define "abomination." The world sure knows what is inappropriate, shouldn't Christians? We must pray God will make His way straight before our face so we will not turn to the right nor the left in compromise (Ps. 5:8; Prov. 4:27).

We must............

walk not as other Gentiles walk, in the vanity of their mind, having their understanding darkened, being alienated from the life of God through the ignorance that is in them, because of the blindness of their heart: who being past feeling, have given themselves over unto lasciviousness, to work all uncleanness with greediness (Eph. 4:17-19).

It is half-hearted to believe strict obedience to God's commands is arrogant and narrow-minded. Perhaps we should repent in sackcloth and ashes for assuming God is flexible concerning righteousness.

It is possible to let our light shine before men so they may see good works which perpetuate the gospel and glorify God's holy character (Matt. 5:16).

Chapter 12

Certainty!

As Christians, there are some things we must nail to the wall and refuse to relinquish. We stand by faith (Rom.11:20). Without faith, it is impossible to please God (Heb. 11:6). It behooves us to know the principles of Christian faith and its foundation.... Jesus, the ROCK. When winds blow and storms come, the rock remains immovable. "Jesus Christ the same yesterday, and today, and forever" (Heb. 13:8). The God of Christianity has "no variableness, neither shadow of turning" (James 1:17). The "foundation of God standeth sure" (2 Tim. 2:19). "Which hope we have as an anchor of the soul, both sure and steadfast" (Heb. 6:19).

Christians do not have to waver when relentless onslaughts of doubt seek to destroy our stance. You can "know the certainty of those things, wherein thou hast been instructed" (Lk. 1:4). God's Word is our guide. "Have I not written to thee excellent things in counsels and knowledge, that I might make thee know the certainty of the words of truth; that thou mightest answer the words of truth to them that send unto thee?" (Prov. 22:20-21).

Questioning

Jude wrote of those who would creep into churches without our knowledge ("unawares") and "deny the ONLY (exclusive) Lord God, and our Lord Jesus Christ" (Jude 4). In verse 11, he foretells, "Woe unto them! for they have gone in the way of Cain" marking them as those who have worshiped God their own way. They have "ran greedily after the error of Balaam" pointing them out as turning the eyes of God's people toward other gods. Finally, the verse reads, they have "perished in the gainsaying of Core" identifying them as rising up in great rebellion against God and His men of faith (See Gen. 4:5; Num. 16: 1-3; Num. 25:1-2; Num. 31:16; Jude 11; Rev. 2:14.)

Ironically, we easily question our grandmother's dogmatic faith, but we aren't questioning skepticism toward truth, divided hearts, or liberal worship practices. Those who accuse saints of the past for hate talk should be looking into the mirror to see where the real negativity lies.

Lately, the hijacking of Christianity's assurance and certainty is evidenced through unprecedented indecisiveness among Christians. Those who have "crept" into the church have generated doubt through "innocent" questioning. Some have made it "sacred" to question foundational beliefs of the church. (See *The Sacredness of Questioning Everything* by David Dark.) Open-ended questioning and indirect answers are intended to create "conversations," but has resulted in doubt and skepticism.

Just as the serpent beguiled Eve in the garden, Satan plants questions about what God really said. Charles Spurgeon who lived in the 1800's, saw the early stages of Satan's final plan when he said he was "sick to death of the common talk about the healthiness of doubting"[1] Doubt has been so elevated as "healthy," that immovable certainty is now considered unhealthy and arrogant.

Discussion is encouraged in our small group settings. We are found asking, "Did God really mean that? Didn't that apply to a different time? Was that translated correctly? Did my parents, who were fundamental in their belief, really teach me the truth? Is Christianity the only truth? Hath God really said, 'Ye shall not eat of every tree of the garden?'"

There is a difference when we question a teacher of God's Word, comparing their words with Scripture and when we question God's Word, doubting its truth. We can doubt people, but we mustn't doubt God. The Bereans in the book of Acts were commended for searching the scriptures in order to answer questions. But unlike the Bereans, questioning today is from a heart of rebellion which refuses God's truth and seeks substitutes.

Interrogating God's Word is like clay questioning the potter. (See Jer. 18:4-6.) It has no right. Man's view of Scripture means nothing, God's intention behind it means everything. While uncertainty about tried and true religion is currently perpetuated, skepticism about new perspectives is not even considered. Paul warned Timothy about those guilty of "knowing nothing, but doting about questions and strifes of words" who are prone to "perverse disputings" (1 Tim. 6:4-5; also 1:4). He also advised him to avoid "foolish and unlearned questions" (2 Tim. 2:23).

Questioning is a diversion. Satan loves for us to spend time in the valley of vague indecision. Week after week, we gain no ground. Since we should not view Scripture according to majority opinion, we must accept God's Word in faith. As Christians are cunningly urged to shift paradigms, we must instead submit without question and hold with confidence the unshifting, absolute truth of God.

The Christian Bible allows no middle ground concerning faith. We cannot treat God's Word as though it's merely opinion. It will "not return void, but it shall accomplish that which" God pleases (Isa. 55:11). Every prophecy, every promise, and every warning will be fulfilled and completed even if we are unaware of it. (See Isa. 14:24.) Christians cannot swallow everything they hear from the pulpit or from Christian literature. Knowing His Word cover to cover helps us decipher when scoffing and mocking comes against it. We can resist the unconvinced, unpersuaded confusion from "emerging" doctrine (2 Pet. 3:3; Jude 18).

As the church is tempted to sympathize with society and culture, the Bible tells us to "cease, my son, to hear the instruction that causeth to err from the words of knowledge" (Prov. 19:27). Paul told the Galatians, "If any man preach any other gospel unto you than that ye have received, let him be accursed" (Gal. 1:9). He goes on to "certify" the gospel is "not after man," but "by the revelation of Jesus Christ" (vs. 11-12). Christians have not only duty, but privilege, to stand devoted to God's Word. (See Ps. 33:8.)

Boasting

Shifting Christianity accuses old-time Christianity of arrogance for boasting in truth and doesn't even notice its arrogance in questioning God and the Bible. The reason exclusive belief in one way to God is considered know-it-all and cocky is because it claims to have the only right answer. But in spite of growing ridicule, Christians must hold their heads high with the psalmist and affirm, "In God we boast all the day long" (Ps. 44:8).

Isn't it Christianity's critics who say recent evolutionary findings show humans will eventually have larger foreheads to accommodate larger brains? This vanity charges Christians with arrogance? Their mirror is darkened and they cannot recognize their vanity. Today's intellectual falls far below those of the past (such as Jonathan Edwards or William Penn) who wrote half-page sentences and used words we have to consult a dictionary to understand.

Humanists praise themselves. But Christians praise truth. Paul told the Corinthians, "For if I have boasted any thing.... I am not ashamed; but as we spake all things to you in truth, even so our boasting, which I made before Titus, is found a truth" (2 Cor. 7:14). Christians can say with conviction, "I know whom I have believed, and am persuaded that he is able to keep that which I have committed unto Him against that day"..... holding "fast the form of sound words..... in faith and love which is in Christ Jesus" (2 Tim. 1:12-13).

Jeremiah's words also encourage us. He was familiar with false doctrine as it wedged into Israel's thinking and caused them to forget God's name. He compared the false prophets' words of his day to the surety of God's words when he asked, "What is the chaff to the wheat?" (Jer. 23:28). As the tide shifts, we can rest assured the battle has already been won and God is not moved even if every person rejected His truth. He doesn't rule by consensus.

Knowing

New religious perspectives paradoxically believe truth cannot be known. Is that a truth itself..... that truth cannot be known? "It is given unto you to know the mysteries of the kingdom of heaven..." (Matt. 13:11). "And ye shall know the truth, and the truth shall make you free" (Jn. 8:32).

Jesus' sheep (Christians) should know His voice when they hear it. Knowing His voice comes only from diligent search of the scriptures. A well-read Christian can more easily decipher when a voice does not match the true voice. A faithful Christian will not follow the wrong person, "but will flee from him: for they know not the voice of strangers" (Jn. 10:4-5). Listening to many voices only breeds confusion.

According to the Bible, we should not even be found with the names of other gods in our mouths, giving them acknowledgment with our words (See Ex. 23:13; Josh. 23:7.) Our reaction to other beliefs (which bare their teeth at truth and the real Christ) should be to "destroy their altars," "break down their images," "cut down their groves," and "burn their graven images with fire" (Deut. 7:5, 26; 2 Chron. 34:7).

This extreme attitude can be our mental disposition and applied individually in our own homes as we rid the premises of anything that honors the gods of this world. It can also be used to teach our children as our reaction utterly rejects false beliefs embedded in other religions. (I am not advocating a physical rampage against other religions. I am speaking to the Christian's responsibility within their own lives and their own homes. If Christians were more steadfast in their own homes, corruption would be less dominant in our society.)

Jeremiah cautioned God's people (Christians) to "learn not the way of the heathen..... for the customs of the people are vain" (Jer. 10:2-3). God commands us to "commit not any one of these abominable customs ... that ye defile not yourselves" (Lev. 18:29-30; 20:23). Learning other methods of worship and caving to the mentality that it is open-minded or even right is abominable to God. God cautioned His people to "inquire not after their gods." Like the Israelites, we are curious, "How did these nations serve their gods? Even so will I do likewise" (Deut. 12:30). Further reading of that text shows us God is very serious. We are to "cleave unto Him" only as we reject acknowledgment of other religions and their practices. (See Deut. 13:4; 20:18).

We, as Christians, are not to associate with customs which identify with witchcraft and idol worship (Deut. 18:9-11). Sadly, there seems to be no resistance among Christians against the influx of evil and supernatural deception. It is a "snare" and can manifest itself in many ways including nightmares, sickness, or even death (Ex. 34:12). "Neither shalt thou bring an abomination into thine house, lest thou be a cursed thing like it: but thou shalt utterly detest it, and thou shalt utterly abhor it; for it is a cursed thing" (Deut. 7:26). Sadly, Old Testament advice is not easily accepted since years of propaganda has told us we should "doubt" its usefulness in our lives.

As Christianity has conceded to other customs, she has found herself trapped. She is currently at the mercy of those who do not believe God's Word. As the jaws clamp around the neck, each Christian is faced with compliance (to release the tension) or defense of God's truths (causing more tension). We have erred because we do not know Scripture (Matt. 22:29). We are refusing to be separate from worldly practices and from clear lines between "us and them." We have made it hard to identify the line between worshiping God according to the Bible and worshiping Him according to opinion. We readily participate in every activity, then walk away without considering the offensive insult to God's holiness.

~~~

Cooperating with other methods, which may help physically but do not benefit spiritually, indicates infidelity. Faithfulness will shun the very appearance of evil, steeling itself in resolve by saying "no" when a practice is associated with pagan practice (1 Thess. 5:22). Psalm 106 teaches us that God's people "did not destroy the nations..... but were mingled among the heathen, and learned their works. And they served their idols: which were a snare unto them" (vs. 34-36). Further reading points to the depravity at the end of this road. "Yea, they sacrificed their sons and their daughters.... and shed innocent blood, even the blood of their sons and of their daughters" (vs. 37-38). Not only is our country guilty of abortion as we acknowledge society's view of right and wrong, but we are spiritually sacrificing children's souls as we embrace other religions which lead them away from true salvation and down various roads to hell.

Satan would struggle to gain a foothold if Christians would only resist by holding to what they know. We must "contend for the faith" and "hold the traditions which we have been taught, whether by word, or epistle" (Jude 3; 2 Thess. 2:15). Christians must stop buckling their knees in apology for overstepping boundaries or walking into territory where they have not been invited. The problem is not the boldness of Christians, but the aggressive nature of indiscretion in our country. If Christians would be militant in their own homes, the battle would not be so hot in the public arena.

We have something to offer which will help people to the saving of their souls. We must be confident and "*know* that the Son of God is come, and hath given us an understanding, that we may *know* Him that is true" (1 Jn. 5:20). We must stop apologizing for truth. Jesus said, "I am the way, the truth, and the life: no man cometh unto the Father, but by me. *If* ye had known me, ye should have known my Father also: and from henceforth ye know Him, and have seen Him" (Jn. 14:6-7). To know Jesus is to know the Father. To see Jesus is to see the real God. But it depends on the "if." We must know *Him* only (not others) to gain eternal life (Jn. 17:3).

~~~

There is a difference in narrow-mindedness which is wrong and narrow belief which is right. Narrow thinking is a good thing when it is applied correctly. We can be glad when a pilot is narrow in his view of destination or he would fly around continually until the plane fell out of the sky from lack of fuel. I'm glad doctors are narrow in their search when they seek to remove an appendix. Otherwise, a person would just be scraped clean of all his vital organs. Radiation only works when narrowly focused on the area to be eradicated. Free radiation kills everything. Narrow thinking in the spiritual realm is even more pertinent.

Social media's advocacy that "all roads" are the same is now an undisputed message. Sources of information are unapologetic in their portrayal that there are no differences and all religions are interchangeable......... so everyone has the *right* to choose whatever his heart desires to worship. This is now fundamental thinking to the younger generation. But the Lord is only near to those who "call upon *Him*, in truth" (Ps. 145:18).

People are searching for truth, yet refusing real truth. They are giving equal time to everything, avoiding the concentrated, narrow attention needed for the right answer. It's like when you're at a stop light, waiting for it to turn green. If you look up then down, left then right, in the glove box, in the back seat, under the driver's seat............. the light turns green and you don't even notice because you're not focusing where you should look. In the mean time, opportunity is missed because the light turns red again. The search in all places for what can only be found in one place is what Paul told Timothy about people who are "ever learning, and never able to come to the knowledge of the truth" (2 Tim. 3:7).

Paul goes on to assure Timothy that even though "evil men and seducers shall wax worse and worse" as time goes by, he should "continue in the things he had learned and been assured of" from his childhood (13-15). We can apply the same principle and remain standing in our Christian belief taught to us in the past before the paradigm shifted and piped for the church to leave its established foundation. (Of course if a person was taught erroneously in his childhood, contrary to God's Word, he should change his thinking. But concerning Christianity as a whole, returning to the beliefs of the early church rather than erasing them is our answer.)

Even Bible-based pastors are beginning to show disapproval for the "churched" and praise the "un-churched" in their congregations. It's to the point where those raised with a godly heritage feel the urge to repent at the altar for holding back the "gathering" from progress and change. Progress now is measured by freedom (to do your own thing). Subliminally, the church is teaching it is better (less arrogant) to wear T-shirts with beer advertisements than shirts with collars when coming into God's presence. Nonetheless, many who were taught respect for God's house should not throw it out just because it's "the old way" or just because they are being "judged" by pragmatists. It's odd how the most strict accuser against judging others is the one who scowls and judges anything associated with old-time Christianity.

So, if we're honest, we have to admit not everyone with a T-shirt and shorts on Sunday morning is a rebel. Nor is everyone in a suit and tie arrogant and self-righteous. But currently, it is obvious which one is receiving criticism in most churches. The assault is not necessarily against surface clothing, but against godly heritage and principles of the past.

Cost of Uncertainty

The high cost of Christian indifference as other means of salvation, other ways of worship, and other perspectives of truth are promoted, will only culminate into lost souls as the broad-minded approach shifts our sons and daughters away from the narrowness of real truth. Scripture warns that a portion of the expense will be paid by church leaders and parents as the Lord is swift to "destroy thee suddenly" for allowing infidelity (Deut. 7:2-5).

God is jealous for our exclusive respect and attention (Ex. 34:14). But churches today face the similar spiritual climate as God's people of Jeremiah's day. We have forgotten God's name and replaced it with the names of other gods. (See Jer. 23:27). We have participated in "creative borrowing" and incorporated other possibilities for Christ. By "burning incense" to other gods, we have filled the land "with the blood of innocents" (Jer. 19:4). By building the "high places of Baal," we are guilty of sacrificing our children to doctrines that will damn their souls (vs.5-6).

Spiritual adultery is disguised as "loving our enemy." As new teachings snatch stray sheep who casually munch on the outskirts of the fold, they shift the whole flock away from truth and toward substitutes. Strays are told the grass is greener the further they wander from boundaries (rules). They are told to let their guard down because there are no wolves (enemies). It's an artful method that leads toward a fatal precipice.

Truth about God's justice and judgment has been rejected because of apparent disagreement with "love." The teaching God is only "love" (with new definition of love embracing everything) has opened our minds to other views of truth. God's love has been taught out of context for so long, many (especially youth) believe it is blasphemous to say anything about God's wrath and judgment.

The fact God's love is actually behind His judgment and justice does not compute with a contemporary mindset. A revised definition has caused "love" to smile at lies and sleep with rattlesnakes. Would we "love" for our child to be kidnapped? No, we would "hate" it because we love our child. True Christians are not hate-mongers for hating evil which threatens people's souls. We must not be afraid to draw the correct line between love and hate and admit God's wrath (past and future) does not contradict His love.

God hates those things which are in opposition to Him (Prov. 6:16-19). God's justice will not allow evil to go unpunished. People who initiate, spread, and ally with evil will be held accountable. We must consider His goodness AND His severity (Rom. 11:22). God is just, fair, and right to penalize those who reject Him. It would be unfair if all went to heaven.

The Lord is "long-suffering to us-ward, not willing that any should perish, but that all should come to repentance" (2 Pet. 3:9). God has provided the way for wicked men (all of us until converted) to escape judgment. God offers a lifeline to help our hopelessness. Rejecting that way is like a drowning man refusing a rope or a caged man refusing a key.

This generation, in general, does not see the need for a rope as it swims in the ocean with everybody else. It does not realize the result of getting too far from the lifeboat. Repercussions are the furthest thing from their minds since society has eliminated lessons about consequences and accountability.

Culture agrees with those in Jeremiah's day who said, "But we will certainly do whatsoever thing goeth forth out of our own mouth" (Jer. 44:17). God's rebuff toward that attitude remains the same, You "shall know whose words shall stand, mine, or theirs" (Jer. 44:28).

The Old Testament is filled with warnings about "enlarging thy bed" with those other than the true God and the resulting consequences of spiritual adultery (Isa. 57:8). Israel's flirtation with other gods (belief systems about right and wrong) caused their "posterity," like ours, to be led away with "fishhooks" until they were slung onto the shore to be gutted without mercy (Amos 4:2).

The bait today (in the world and the church) is very appealing because it is coated with inclusive "love." To love and embrace all cars, without exclusion, causes the shopper to purchase a lemon. To love and embrace all medicines, without distinction, causes the swallower to get over-dosed or over-medicated. To love and embrace all round things as fruit finds the eater rushed to the ER to extract a baseball from his throat. The "no wrong answer" curriculum dispensed to our children has caused them to grasp anything without discretion. We have left them uninformed and unprotected.

How has the church fallen off the cliff and into a faulty paradigm? First, we followed the crowd by walking to the edge just to have a casual look. We didn't want to be judgmental, so we didn't walk away. Now we find ourselves in adultery with other religions because after following the crowd just to look, we listened, flirted, then lay down without a fight.

We've courted other views, and now the affair is consummated with beliefs such as pantheism, evolution, psychology, yoga, "stream of consciousness," consciousness-raising techniques, eastern meditation, visualization and hypnosis, acupuncture, biofeedback, guided imagery, karma, human potential, the "real you" (as basically good), energy alignment, goddess within, Mother Earth, Harry Potter, near-death experiences (as spiritual encounters with other spirits), Kabbalah, healing stones and crystals, centering, "meditation," visualization, channeling, paranormal activities, reincarnation, energy flow/imbalance, lucid dreaming, music meditation, drugs, "the force," yin-yang, peace signs, color therapy, aromatherapy, pagan festivals, "all roads lead to heaven," "there are no wrong answers," putting differences aside (spiritual), environmentalism (when creation is above Creator), mystical experiences, psychic phenomenon, sensuality, "God is only love," tolerance (beyond its limits), community-minded (when misapplied spiritually), "collective strength," the Universal Mind, brotherhood of man, coexistence, inclusive (beyond its limit), unity in diversity, "dialogue," "the conversation," integration, "sharing," "convergence," interconnectedness, interdependence, "encountering," "group dynamics," theory, tribalization, atheism, secularism, humanism, universality, global-minded, culture transformation.................

Many of the previous terms from world religions are used in Christianity. But more specifically, postmodern Christian vocabulary and practice include the following: experiential worship, contemplative prayer, contemplative silence, meditative silence, liturgical, repetitive prayer and chants, monasticism, "ancient," Taize worship, worship "gathering," strobe lights, creative lighting, incense and candles or even darkness, mist/fog, multi-sensory worship (seeing, hearing, tasting, smelling, touching, and experiencing.) There was definitely incense in the tabernacle, but its perfume was not common, nor was it used by anyone in any place. See Ex. 30:34-38; Isa. 65:3; see also Ezek. 8:12.), expression worship (through art, photography, sculpture, poetry), peaceful nature scenes, imagery, social gospel, justice movement, missional (without repentance), pluralism, plurality of truth, "partnering" (can be used correctly or incorrectly), re-imagine, ecumenical cooperation (with all religions), at-one-ment; Kingdom of God (out of context and through men's efforts), reign of God, community of God, story of God, redemptive (out of context), paradigm shift, emergence...... and new meanings and definitions for: love, sin, repentance, witness, salvation, redemption, rebellion, and ultimately.............. perverting the name of Jesus by inserting others in His place .....such as Imam Mahdi, Krishna, Buddha, Mohammed, or Maitreya (Deut. 11:16; Hos. 4:12; Isa. 57:4-5; Jer. 3:6).

Individual Christians must consider their actions and resist the "culture of participation" and the current spiritual phenomenon whether it proceeds from the mouth of their entertainment or from their pastor. Isaiah told God's people they had "shut their eyes, that they cannot see; and their hearts, that they cannot understand" (Isa. 44:18). "None considereth in their heart" that they have been unfaithful to their husband (Jesus) (Isa. 44:19).

Coerced by society, few judge right from wrong in spiritual matters. Christians aren't, for the most part, saying "no" or drawing clear lines. It's difficult and out-of-date to be on the outskirts of social media's "dialogue." The Bible advises, "discretion shall preserve thee" (Prov. 2:11). We would be wise to re-evaluate our time spent with diversions and shun the notion we are entitled to what makes us happy.

Jeremiah wrote how God's people said, "I am innocent" and "I have not sinned." The Lord "rejected their confidences" (Jer. 2:35-37). God was repulsed as He told Israel, "Thou hast... increased thy whoredoms, to provoke me to anger" (Ezek. 16:26; Isa. 57:8; Hos. 5:4). God rejecting our excuses is foreign to our mentality. We aren't familiar with His attributes which demand justice (what we deserve from His perspective not what we deserve from our perspective). In fact, we live as if we "refuse to know" God (Jer. 9:6). It is this lack of information about Him that causes us to be silent when we should speak up on His behalf. We say nothing because we have nothing to say.

"My people..... are not valiant for the truth upon the earth" (Jer. 7:28, 9:2-3). If only Christians were valiant for truth. What a difference we would see in our culture! The current fight for righteousness in our government (state and federal) has resulted from our lack of vigilance in our own homes.

Solid Faith

The result of *spiritual* adultery is a generation of spiritual bastards, illegitimately fathered by any trend that sweeps our culture. Children, for the most part, do not belong to the one true Father. (This applies directly to those children brought up in churches sympathetic to postmodern thought.) As new definitions for biblical terms shift, understanding is no longer founded upon real meanings, and thus belief is bypassed and salvation thwarted.

An attempt to revive the "ancient" way is but an appearance of returning to biblical foundations. It brings back old hymns which have been dormant long enough for semantics to change. Words like redemption, grace, hell, salvation, and repentance are now interpreted through dark lenses. Hymns that once converted the sinner to the narrow way, now only unite all who sing them under the broad banner of love. Singers assume the lyrics apply to everyone rather than to Christians alone. The church must mend her broken nets and realize "fish" will not be caught for the kingdom with something which may be called a "net" or even look like a net, but in reality, is a great big hula hoop.

The shift in gospel meaning is quickly on track for a complete new method of operation. J. Lee Grady, contributing editor for Charisma magazine, stated, "The doctrines of heaven, hell, salvation and damnation are too serious to be treated haphazardly. May the Lord help us reclaim a truly New Testament gospel in this hour of spiritual compromise."[2]

~~~

Yes, this generation is hurting and facing problems like never before. Turning their attention onto physical problems does not help. Temporary help is not the answer. Turning their eyes to spiritual truth is their hope. God is a "father to the fatherless" and He is their only solution (Ps. 43:5; 68:5). The children in our churches require life-changing answers. We must stop bandaging troubles with humanistic approaches. We must go deeper than surface "love and compassion." We must seek to rebuild crumbling foundations. Faith in narrow truth must be renewed while faith in empty alternatives must be rejected.

According to the dictionary, "faith" is a trust, a confidence, and a complete acceptance of a truth which includes loyalty, steadfastness, and being true to the original.[3] Against the tide of strong deception, believers must be stronger than ever, holding fast with loyalty and steadfastness to things we know to be true. Lifelines for our children are slipping away until they will be completely withheld from their reach. True faith includes being "true to the original" (not what we're told is ancient and biblical, yet proves to be false). Faith is not true if it puts confidence in all sources, just in case one fails. Trusting in back-up systems is not commitment.

Charles Spurgeon's sermon entitled, "On the Cross After Death" describes the fulfillment of prophecies concerning Jesus. The fact none of Jesus' bones were broken on the cross, yet His side was pierced is only one example of the sureness of God's prophecy. (See Ps. 22:16; Ps. 34:20.) Even with the soldiers' free will, God accomplished what had been prophesied years before. Not one bone of The Word was broken even when the soldiers broke the legs of the other two men.

We cannot allow the foundational structure (bones) of the Word (Jesus) be broken by our shifts in doctrine. Even as there are those who seek to distort and take away its truth, our faith can be built upon steadfast surety. We can stand on the Rock and say with David, "I shall not be moved" (Ps. 16:8). We can agree with the hymn, *On Christ the Solid Rock I Stand*. All other religions are sinking sand.

Spurgeon speaks of the Christian faith being founded on rock-solid certainty:

> Faith loves not slippery places; faith seeks the sure word of prophecy, and sets her foot firmly upon certainties. Unless all the Word of God is sure, and pure 'as silver tried in a furnace of earth, purified seven times,' then we have nothing to go upon. If I am to take the Bible and say, 'Some of this is true, and some of it is questionable,' I am no better off than if I had no Bible.... It would be a happy circumstance if the childlike reverence of the early fathers could

> be restored to the church, and the present irreverent
> criticism could be repented of and cast away.[4]

It's sobering to read the Bible and see God takes Christian faith very
seriously. We find that "if we hold the beginning of our confidence
steadfast unto the end," we will be made "partakers of Christ" (Heb.
3:14). We are instructed to "hold fast the profession of our faith without wavering" (Heb. 10:23). Society is so muddled with flexibility
of opinion and new meaning for long-held belief that many do not
even detect wavering. All the while, Satan lures the teetering masses
further and further down toward irreversible destruction.

~~~

My stand against compromise does not advocate the belief that
Christian's can lose their salvation. My concern is if "Christians" are
saved in the first place based on their loyalty versus what they say
they believe. It is a different book altogether to speak of Christians
whose hearts truly seek to please God, yet are imperfect. Real
Christians can be grateful for grace and blood which covers all.

We must pray this generation will not follow the false christ who is
incompatible with Scripture. We must teach them to know the *real*
Jesus literally, physically, spiritually, and personally. He alone fits
every description of the Christ of the Bible. We must teach boldness
and certainty in our proclamation of faith. Instead of an "all is one"
interpretation of life, we must see that "all is all" and "one is one"
meaning *all* religions will bow to the *one* true religion of Christianity
with a vivid line of division between.

Faltering away from what Christianity knows to be true is a very
serious predicament. Satan is not haphazardly attacking us, but
going for the throat as he stirs doubt causing us to withdraw from
the line once held with surety. A faithful Christian remains loyal to
the belief that his relationship to God is only through Jesus, known
only through one source....... the Bible. He realizes his relationship

is not an easy come, easy go matter. (Interesting note: In Roget's Thesaurus, "easy come, easy go" is in the same list as "prodigal.")

When critical issues are at stake, the church must discern between error and truth and not shy away from clearly stating what is wrong and what is right. Validity of speakers should be judged by God's Word. Mere opinion should not be the judge. The number of "likes" on facebook only shows tolerance, not necessarily discernment. Christians can be deceived now more than ever as we approach the end of the church era. Satan will persevere until his puppet is in place of world dominance.

~~~

Satan colorfully paints his way of death with images of light and life (2 Cor. 11:14). But God sends prophets to His people to point them back to truth. He doesn't leave them groping and hopeless. God sets before us life and death, blessing and cursing. He tells us to choose life (Deut. 30:19).

We are commanded to be:

> courageous to keep and do all that is written ... that
> we turn not aside therefrom to the right hand or to the
> left..... neither make mention of the name of their gods,
> nor cause to swear by them, neither serve them, nor
> bow ..... but cleave unto the Lord our God (Josh. 23:6-8).

"Cleaving" to truth does not include throwing an arm around another belief or even tolerating different practices. An adulterer may claim to adhere to his wife while winking at others, but he still earns the name "cheater." A woman may say she loves her husband while she texts all her old boyfriends, but she is not the devoted wife she pretends to be.

Man's choice, spiritually, is one or all. If he decides to choose all, he soon finds he has none. If he wants life, he must choose the specific, narrow way and forsake all others. How sad for people on Judgment Day to really believe they are Christian, but realize Christianity was just *one* of their "husbands." Fatally, He was not their only one.

We must realize the authority of God's Word whereby we will be judged. We will not be judged according to man's idea of truth no matter the unanimity.... no matter what has been voted legal or illegal...... no matter how many states allow it. Belief in truth is proven by action or lack of action. I believe fire burns, so I don't stick my hand in it....... ever. I believe it's unsafe to sleep in the street, so you won't find me setting up a tent there...... ever. Jesus words in red are, "He that rejecteth me, and receiveth not my words, hath one that judgeth him: *the word* that I have spoken, the same shall judge him in the last day" (Jn. 12:48). Let's not ignore those very words written in the Holy Bible.

God is not affected by lies. He is not shaken by false religions. He remains true, steadfast, and perfect through it all. (See Deut. 32:4; 2 Tim. 2:18-19; Isa. 40:17.) His truth is set in stone, never to be changed or adapted to fit people. It is man who must change and adapt to Him. Christians must wave a banner in their hearts proclaiming, "For all people will walk every one in the name of his god, and we will walk in the name of the Lord our God forever and ever" (Mic. 4:5). The church must remain separate from the world and love what God loves and hate what He hates, discerning good from evil. The world will listen when they see a difference.

Truth cannot change, cannot be renamed, cannot have different meanings, and cannot come from different perspectives. *There is a difference* between the "old-fashioned" gospel and the new postmodern gospel, between the old rugged cross and the mass-marketed, glitzy, gaudy cross. *There's a difference* between the narrow way and the broad, inclusive way. *There is a difference* between long-standing truth and emerging lies. Jesus is coming back for a faithful remnant.

~~~

Delusion gets stronger as the "new Jesus" fits all creeds. There is a false "oneness" in the name of a hybrid christ. The new "one" includes many. One is now all humanity (visibly) or even all "human love" (invisibly). "One" cannot be "many." People can never unify under everything. True "oneness" or unity can only be in the specificity of Jesus. Only Jesus is the true Messiah, the man who died on the cross and rose the third day. Prophetic verses apply to Him selectively. He only fulfilled every prophecy. Point-blank Scripture only fits Him. Only *that* man is God. Only through Him is there access to the Father, eternal life, redemption, and salvation. He is the *one* Savior for all mankind. ("All" means those who believe and obey what HE has said in His Word.) In "the fullness of times, He [will] gather together in *one* all things *in Christ*, both which are in heaven, and which are on earth" (Eph. 1:10).

There are two groups: Those who are unified to God through *the Christ of the Bible* and those who are separated from God (and from the first group) because of their rejection of *the Christ of the Bible.* How can these two opposite groups be united? Only in presumption. There are two churches: The church of Jesus and the church of Satan. Men remain in Satan's church until they go through the only door of escape (Jn. 10:9). Satan doesn't have to convert men to his side, he only has to keep them from escaping. He distracts them away from the true door. He lies about the door. He builds fake doors to look like the real door, but those who go through find themselves falling into a burning lake of fire on the other side.

So shrewd at deception and unwilling to give up, Satan has even formed the lie of all lies—He now is pointing to the right Door (through false teachers) and says, "You don't have to go *through* the door because it's *wide* enough that it already embraces you in love. It would never leave anyone out of its inclusiveness. Just stay where you are and feel the love." Then a person is tricked if he doesn't, by an act of his will, go through the narrow door and into life.

Two suppers prepared by God at the end of time are mentioned in Revelation 19. There is the "marriage supper of the Lamb" and the "supper of the great God" (vs. 9, 17). There are irreconcilable differences between the two when you consider who is invited to each. "Blessed are they which are called unto the marriage supper of the Lamb" while those invited to the "other" supper find themselves on the menu. "All the fowls are filled with their flesh" (vs. 9, 21).

Current preaching about an earthly kingdom must be discerned to be either the Millennial kingdom of Jesus or the Antichrist's kingdom which will have "democratic" (but in reality, dictatorial) answers for global problems. The impostor and those perpetuating his agenda will use all the right words and quote all the right people, but his program will be puzzling, deliberately veiled in meaning, and hard to define. He will not seem to be in opposition to Christ or appear to be against God. But as the greatest insurgent ever, he will claim to be God Himself (2 Thess. 2:3-4). The Antichrist will seek his own glory rather than the glory of the Father. (See Jn. 7:18.) He will strive to go higher and higher *up* in his arrogance...... yet another disparity between him and the true Christ who came *down* lower as He placed Himself in the humble position of human flesh.

When hearing about salvation, redemption, justice, and "rebellion" in our churches, we must discern which definition fits God's definition. We must know the right one, established from the beginning. Even when polished words are used, we must know if the application is crafted for global unity under "one" banner of humanism or unified under "one" banner of Christ.

> And the Lord shall be king over all the earth: in that day shall there be *one* Lord, and His name *one* (Zech. 14:9).

> Hear, O Israel: The Lord our God is *one* Lord (Deut. 6:4).

> For there is *one* God, and *one* mediator between God
> and men, the man Christ Jesus (1 Tim. 2:5).

Know what is meant by "one." It is not plural or inclusive. Jesus is not a "consciousness," an "awareness," a "state of mind," or a "way of empathizing with humanity." These intangible smoke screens are not the man who came in the *flesh* to take the punishment for man's guilt, becoming the door to eternal life for those who accept that truth. (See 1 Jn. 4:2-3; 2 Jn. 7). True Christians accept Jesus as He is and do not expect Him to fit their own unique experience.

I pray we become extremely uncomfortable with our complacency toward truth. I pray we clearly draw a line which separates truth from lies. May the Holy Spirit prick our conscience until we no longer shrug our shoulders toward shades of gray. I pray we are bold for Christ's name's sake and for the sake of this generation who is in desperate need of the saving knowledge of Jesus Christ.

Let

every

kindred,

every tribe

on this terrestrial ball

to Him

all majesty ascribe

and crown Him

Lord of all.[5]

Endnotes

Chapter 1 The Paradigm Shift

1 Amy Green, "Churches Add 'Creation Care' to Social Agenda," *Charisma*, April 2010, 18.
Jennifer Toledo, "Emerging Leaders," *Charisma*, April 2010, 33.
J. Lee Grady, "Passing the Torch," *Charisma*, April 2010, 66.
2 Brian D. McLaren, *A Generous Orthodoxy* (Grand Rapids, MI: Zondervan, 2004), 316-317.
3 Ibid., 152.
4 Amy Becker Williams, "Dueling beliefs? Group sees vastly differing religions as complementary," *Amarillo Globe News,* Sept. 25, 2010.
5 James Hallmark, "Two faiths join for a meal," *Amarillo Globe News*, May 8, 2010.

Chapter 2 Discernment

1 John MacArthur, *The Jesus You Can't Ignore* (Nashville, TN: Thomas Nelson, 2008), xxi.
2 *Webster's Dictionary of the English Language* (New York, NY: Lexicon Publications, Inc., 1989), s.v. "charity."
3 K.P. Yohannan, *Revolution in World Missions* (Carrollton, TX: gfa books, 2004), 103.
4 Ibid., 102.
5 Ibid., 103.
6 Ibid., 104.
7 Ibid., 105.
8 Ibid.

9   Ibid.

10 Ibid., 106.

11 Franklin Graham, *Rebel With a Cause* (Nashville, TN: Thomas Nelson, 1995), 187.

Chapter 3 The Postmodern Twist

1   *Webster's Dictionary of the English Language,* s.v. "unity."

2   Kester Brewin, *Signs of Emergence* (Grand Rapids, MI: Baker Books, 2007), 198.

3   Samir Selmanovic, *An Emergent Manifesto* (Grand Rapids, MI: Baker Books, 2007), 192.

4   *Webster's Dictionary of the English Language,* s.v. "religion."

Chapter 4 What's the Difference?

1   Kester Brewin, *Signs of Emergence* (Grand Rapids, MI: Baker Books, 2007), 167.

2   Ibid., 183.

3   Ibid., 195.

4   Ibid., 197.

5   Ibid.

6   Ibid., 196.

7   John MacArthur, *The Truth War* (Nashville, TN: Thomas Nelson, 2007), 7.

8   Dr. Sanjiv Chopra and Fr. Alan Lotvin, *Dr. Chopra Says* (New York, NY: St. Martin's Press, 2010), 298.

9   Russill Paul, *The Yoga of Sound* (Novato, CA: New World Library, 2004), 16.

10 Ibid., 209.

11 Ibid.

Chapter 5 Divided Heart

1   Kari Jobe, "Untainted Love," *Charisma,* April 2011, 65.

2   *Roget's International Thesaurus* (New York, NY: Harper & Row, Publishers, 1977), s.v. "contaminate."

Chapter 7 How the Paradigm Shifted

1   Dan Kimball, *Emerging Worship* (Grand Rapids, MI: Zondervan, 2004), 218.

2   Alistair Begg, Truth for Life Ministries (Cleveland, OH: 2010), Radio by Grace, 88.7 Amarillo, TX, July 21, 2010.

3   "'Nones' on the Rise," Pew Research, Oct. 9.2012, http://www.pewforum.org/2012/10/09/nones-on-the-rise (accessed 28 Aug 2013).

4   Leonard Pitts, Jr., "Rice keeps faith, but loses religion," *Amarillo Globe News*, Aug. 5, 2010.

5   Brian D. McLaren, *A Generous Orthodoxy* (Grand Rapids, MI: Zondervan, 2004), 87.

6   *Webster's Dictionary of the English Language*, s.v. "contend."

7   David Jeremiah, *I Never Thought I'd See the Day!* (New York, NY: Faith Words, 2011), 49.

8   A.W. Tozer, *Tozer on Worship and Entertainment* (Camp Hill, PA: Christian Publications, 1997), 95.

9   *Good Morning America,* WWII vet story, July 5, 2009.

10 Samir Selmanovic, *An Emergent Manifesto* (Grand Rapids, MI: Baker Books, 2007), 193-194.

11 Ibid., 315.

12 J. Lee Grady, "A Squishy Gospel," *Charisma*, July 2011, 66.

13 *Webster's Dictionary of the English Language*, s.v. "truth."

Chapter 8 Embracing Other Religions

1   "Many Americans say other faiths can lead to eternal life," Pew Research, Dec. 18, 2008, http://www.pewforum.org/2008/12/18 (Accessed 9 Aug 2013).

2   Brian Zahnd, "End of the Line," *Charisma*, May 2010, 47.

3   Ibid., 47.

4   Ibid., 48.

5 Ibid.

6 Barry Taylor, *An Emergent Manifesto* (Grand Rapids, MI: Baker Books, 2007), 168-169.

7 Samir Selmanovic, *An Emergent Manifesto* (Grand Rapids, MI: Baker Books, 2007), 191.

8 Terry Muck and Frances S. Adeney, *Christianity Encountering World Religions* (Grand Rapids, MI: Baker Books, 2009), 48.

9 Ibid., 49.

10 Kathleen Parker, "Pray to which God?," *Amarillo Globe News*, May 9, 2010.

11 Ibid.

12 Charles Spurgeon, "Knowledge, Worship, Gratitude," *The Treasury of the Bible*, Vol. 6 (Grand Rapids, MI: Baker Books, reprint 1981), 885.

13 *Webster's Dictionary of the English Language*, s.v. "emerge."

Chapter 9 The Exclusiveness of Jesus

1 Transcript of remarks delivered by former President William Jefferson Clinton at Georgetown University, November 7, 2001. www.georgetown.edu/admin/publicaffairs/protocol

2 Brian D. McLaren, *A Search for What is Real* (Grand Rapids, MI:Zondervan, 2007), 72.

3 Ibid., 17.

4 Ibid., 181.

5 Merrill Unger, *The New Unger's Bible Dictionary* (Chicago, IL: Moody Press, 1988), 174.

6 Stuart Townsend and Keith Getty, *In Christ Alone*, 2002.

Chapter 10 Impersonator

1 David Jeremiah, *What in the World is Going On?* (Nashville, TN: Thomas Nelson, 2008), 157.

2 Ibid.

3 John MacArthur, *The Truth War* (Nashville, TN: Thomas Nelson, 2007), xiii.

4   Ibid., xxiv.

Chapter 11 Spiritual Compromise

1   A. W. Tozer, *The Quotable Tozer 1* (Camp Hill, PA: Christian
     Publications, 1984), 178.
2   *Webster's Dictionary of the English Language,* s.v. "tolerance."
3   *Roget's International Thesaurus,* s.v. "tolerance."
4   Eldon K. Winker, *The New Age is Lying to You* (St. Louis, MO:
     Concordia, 1994), 139.
5   A. W. Tozer, *The Quotable Tozer 1* (Camp Hill, PA: Christian
     Publications, 1984), 19.
6   Rabbi Daniel Lapin, *America's Real War* (Sisters, OR: Multnomah,
     1999), 210.

Chapter 12 Certainty!

1   Charles Spurgeon, "The Three Witnesses," *The Treasury of the
     Bible*, Vol. 8 (Grand Rapids, MI: Baker Books, 1981), 590.
2   J. Lee Grady, "A Squishy Gospel," *Charisma*, July 2011, 66.
3   *Webster's Dictionary of the English Language,* s.v. "faith."
4   Charles Spurgeon, "On the Cross After Death," *Treasury of the
     Bible*, Vol. 6 (Grand Rapids, MI: Baker Books, 1981), 678-679.
5   Edward Perronet, *All Hail the Power of Jesus Name!*, 1779.

Printed in the United States
By Bookmasters